THE OFFICE STYLE BOOK

BY JUDITH PRICE

DESIGNED BY BOB CIANO

HARMONY BOOKS/NEW YORK

Published by Harmony Books, a division of Crown Publishers, Inc.,
One Park Avenue, New York, New York 10016
and simultaneously in Canada by General Publishing Limited
by arrangement with the Linden Press/Simon & Schuster,
a Division of Gulf & Western Corporation.
HARMONY BOOKS and colophon are trademarks of Crown Publishers, Inc.

Previously published as *Executive Style*

Manufactured in the United States of America

Designed by Bob Ciano

Library of Congress Cataloging in Publication Data

Price, Judith, 1942–
The office style book.

Originally published: Executive style.
New York: Linden Press, 1980.
1. Office decoration.   2. Executives.
I. Title.
NK2195.04P74   1982   747'.852   82-11912

ISBN: 0-517-547171

1 3 5 7 9 10 8 6 4 2

First Paperback Edition

ACKNOWLEDGMENTS

I want to thank all the executives who graciously allowed us to feature their offices in this book. And to convey my thanks to all the architects, designers, manufacuturers, wholesalers and retailers who patiently answered my questions and offered advice and direction.

My particular thanks to the photographers whose pictures appear on the following pages and to the man who led us to them, Melvin L. Scott. To Henry Groskinsky (pages 12–26, 27 bottom, 54–71, 94–101, 108–111, 114, 115, 134–137, 140–145, 152, 153, 168–175, 182–187, 192, 193); Harry Benson (pages 11, 30, 31, 34, 36–39, 45–47, 50, 51, 75, 79, 88, 89, 90, 91, 117, 122–127, 130, 131, 133, 160–165, 167, 194–213 and end papers, front and back); Jerry Sarapochiello (pages 35, 40, 41, 43, 44, 72, 73, 74, 80, 81, 93, 116, 118–121); Michael Pateman (pages 32, 33, 48, 49, 53, 76–78, 84–87); Larry Dale Gordon (pages 112, 113, 146–149); Jim Leviton (pages 28, 29, 106, 107); Arnold Zann (pages 27 top, 104, 105, 178–181, 188–191); Tom Tracy (pages 138, 139); Jim Olive (pages 176, 177); Carl Fischer (pages 82, 83, 128, 129); Jaime Ardiles-Arce (pages 156–159); Richard Payne (pages 102, 103) and Jeffrey Folinus (pages 150, 151, 154, 155).

To Mallory Samson, my research assistant, who supervised many a photography session and kept me constantly organized.

To Mary Dunphy and Grace Karl for their seemingly endless supply of staunch support and tireless assistance, and to Madlyn Deming for being on call for all the last-minute details.

A special thanks to Joni Evans, my editor, who provided the necessary faith and cheered me on the finish.

And, of course, to Bob Ciano, whose good taste and superb design have helped to make this book what it is.

—Judith Price

CONTENTS

Any successful company has known about style for years. Style makes whatever you sell distinctive—and better than somebody else's product. Style is quality, innovation; but it's also design, advertising, packaging. It's what makes your company and its product stand out in a crowd. ☐ The chairman or president, designer or director behind a product can stand out, too. Executive style need not be blatant—unless you're a Rothschild and can afford to keep a functioning spittoon in your office, or, like power pundit Michael Korda, you make the rules and therefore can break them. (Mr. Korda's decor features a collection of helmets and a gallery of equestrian memorabilia.) But neither is it simply good taste or design. "An ax handle doesn't have style," said Mies van der Rohe. "It has beauty and appropriateness of form and a this-is-how-it-should-be-ness, but it has no style because style reflects idiosyncrasies." Style is certainly not just money: A thousand-dollar attaché case with a designer's initials on it doesn't have much style at all. ☐ Style isn't something you're born with or something you acquire when you reach a certain age. It isn't something you earn if you live in a particular city or at a specific address. Style comes only from recognizing your own best traits and exhibiting them with taste and flair in everything you do. Style is what makes whoever you meet know you are unique. ☐ Executive style shows up in everything you as a successful executive do—the way you entertain, the way you travel, the team you hire. But one part of your work life conveys executive style better than anything else: your office. Not long ago, most executives thought that caring about how an office looked was frivolous, money-wasting, unbusinesslike. But most executives didn't care what color shirt they wore, either, so long as it was white, or about the length of their hair, so long as it was the same as everybody else's. ☐ Now in even the most conservative professions, that corporate uniform has come to mark its wearer for what he is: bland, boring, and behind the times. A good executive, says management expert Peter Drucker, exists to make sensible exceptions to general rules. That makes executives with style neither followers nor outsiders, but leaders—confident and decisive. People succeeding in business today know how to distinguish themselves, and they know that one place to do that with style is in the room where they work. Not that they're running to decorators for the latest in Ultrasuede couches. Indeed, executive style may ignore trends altogether: David Rockefeller's office has stayed the same since 1961.

An office with executive style harmonizes with the image of the company while it lets you show your individuality. Never is it overdecorated. It must set you off but not dominate you, reflect you but not overpower you. An office should be a *frame* for your personality; a giant desk or a massive chair, for example, makes so strong a statement it pushes you out of the picture. A raft of family photographs may transmit too much intimacy; a wall full of diplomas and awards signals insecurity to more people than it impresses. □ Your office should be a happy and comfortable place. It should force you to be more creative, more energetic. It should tell everyone who walks in—your boss, your colleagues, your staff, your clients—that you care about your work. Above all, your office should be a haven. Management experts estimate that executives spend twice as many of their waking hours in their offices as they do in their homes. Your spouse's tastes aren't reflected here, or your kids' fingermarks, or your dog's hair. Even if your furniture is regulation-issue, you can make your office your own and make your mark with style. Style can be a daisy in a vase, a cushion on a couch, sandwiches served on a black lacquer tray instead of a cardboard carton. If you're lucky enough to have money and freedom, style can be anything you want it to be. □ The offices and objects pictured in this book prove that style isn't a matter of office size or size of budget, of period of furniture or brand of carpeting. Each office in this book showcases an individual—from Estée Lauder with her drawing-room romanticism to the captain's-bridge sleekness of Oppenheimer & Company's chairman, Jack Nash. The rooms were chosen from nearly a thousand offices suggested by leading architectural and design firms across the country, and were selected in consultation with leaders of the architectural and design community. Unlike catalogues of office furniture, the presentation here ranges across periods, manufacturers, and styles (although, like a catalogue, it does include a directory, with prices as current as inflation permits). □ Yet *The Office Style Book* is not a book about interior decorating. Instead, it's a book about exterior reflection. Not every desk or chair or table, attaché case or fountain pen would be right for who you are—that's just the point of executive style. But every object has the clean lines and good design that project strength, directness, and competence, the basis on which you as an executive can build your own individual style.

DESKS

Not so long ago, executives chose their desks from catalogues the way they chose paper clips and pens, selecting from an assembly-line assortment of big, bulky Executive Model 1000s, V.I.P. 2001s. Those massive monoliths were designed to shout "Important!" Trouble was, they upstaged the V.I.P. executive in the chair behind them. The desk most popular today with successful executives is lean and strong, with few or no drawers and no files, cubbyholes, or cabinets. In fact, today's desk looks more like a table. Many of the executives whose offices are pictured here use theirs as a conference table, or choose to forgo a desk entirely. Whatever working surface they use, though, is streamlined to set off the person behind it. Yours should be functional (if you can't be parted from your papers, consider built-in wall units or a credenza in your work area). Desk or table, your work surface should convey strength and substance. Wood is excellent at projecting those qualities. Other materials—stone, steel, leather, even Formica and glass—can establish distinction without dandyism.

Does that mean you have to spend a fortune for a desk? Not really, though here, as everywhere, you get what you pay for. Look for clean lines and honest design and materials. What doesn't convey solidity and propriety is a material that tries to be something it's not—Naugahyde that's masquerading as leather, plastic that's trying (and failing) to be wood. If you're after a traditional desk, though, don't turn up your nose at reproductions. Distressed wood, which badly counterfeits the look of an antique, is the sort of thing you want to avoid. But a careful reproduction, constructed of good materials, is to be considered if you can't afford an original design of the past.

Bob Fomon, Chief Executive Officer of E. F. Hutton & Company, the country's second-largest brokerage house, can't be pinned down to one desk. Three areas create three different office environments, and three table shapes serve different needs. An antique Regency desk anchors the room; in contrast, a contemporary rosewood and lacquer table for the formal conference area; and finally, a honed granite and Kortan steel coffee table for the informal meeting area. The unexpected use of the Pirelli rubber tile floor with the antique Heriz is both practical—Mr. Fomon loves to pace—and elegant.

An office doesn't have to be large to be grand. It doesn't even have to have a window. But what furniture there is in the office, above, of Erwin Isman, President of Perry Ellis Sportswear, is choice—chairs designed by Eames and Mies van der Rohe, and a hand-lacquered English sycamore desk that achieves the proportions of sculpture. The offices had formerly been a bank, and the marble column behind Mr. Isman's desk was deservedly retained to enhance this environment. The tinted glass walls give light and privacy in one stroke, and also enlarge the room. At right, Mr. Isman's secretary's office prepares the visitor for the understated elegance that lies behind his office door.

In 1917, Mrs. Morton Plant traded her townhouse on Fifth Avenue and Fifty-second Street in Manhattan to Cartier for a string of pearls valued at one million dollars. The mansion now houses the office of Cartier president Ralph Destino, in a room that preserves without embalming its original grandeur. Mr. Destino's desk and desk chairs demonstrate that rules about gender aren't sacred when it comes to choosing office furniture. The elegant Louis Quinze-styled desk and desk chairs are undeniably masculine, belying the notion that French furniture goes best in the boudoir. Nor must one follow outdated rules against mixing periods—the contemporary upholstered club chair by the window blends in perfectly. The Cartier plaque was once on the façade of the building. (Cartier, incidentally, got the better of that trade with Mrs. Plant. With the advent of cultured pearls, prices plummeted, and at her death in 1956, Mrs. Plant's pearls fetched some $150,000 at auction.)

The desk pictured here is the most massive in this book, but Walter Hoving, chairman of Tiffany & Co., wouldn't be dwarfed by a redwood. The eighteenth-century mahogany partners' desk is flanked by three Chippendale armchairs; the bowls on the desk are Lowestoft, and the box and engagement book cover are vermeil. The wood paneling and overhead light lend an aura of strength and permanence.

If ever an office expressed its occupant's taste, it's that of cosmetics czarina Estée Lauder, and only a secure personality (that is, someone who owns the show) can afford quite this much individuality. But the result here is glorious—a lush, opulent office that outshines the most luxurious drawing rooms. The Louis XVI desk is the centerpiece of a salon that mixes European periods, patterns, furniture, and accessories. The walls, covered with hand-painted Oriental rice paper, add to the effect.

On this page, we see Mrs. Lauder's desk as we enter the room. The draperies, inspired by the Schönbrunn Palace in Vienna, frame a spectacular view of Central Park. Who would know we were in New York's modern General Motors skyscraper?

At right is one of the few displays of awards that do more for the observer's eye than for the owner's ego. Usually, displays of awards, diplomas, family pictures and the like have no place in the executive office. But these accolades of crystal and glass are the exception.

23

The office of Ira Howard Levy, Senior Vice President of Corporate Marketing-Design of Estée Lauder, is centuries removed in feeling from his boss's, but no less arresting. Mr. Levy uses small space to optimum advantage, choosing each detail with exacting discernment. The cantilevered desk attests to the maxim that less is more. From the front, one would not imagine this trim desk could support the luxury of a drawer (pictured above). The desk chair is upholstered in seal-colored Hermes leather. All this perfection has not made Mr. Levy lose his touch of humor. The screwdriver sculpture is a touch of whimsy that some, if not all, offices could tolerate.

Three very different offices with three very different desks—yet all of them work in their environment, functionally and as elements of design. At left is the office of United Match Corporation's chairman and president, H. Ridgely Bullock. Here the mahogany, eighteenth-century-styled English desk echoes its traditional surroundings. At top right is the Chicago office of Banco di Roma's chairman, John T. Rettaliata. The desk here is of African rosewood trimmed in polished stainless steel, repeating the straight and geometric lines of the office. (Square and round desks are unusual in that they have no designated "power seat"; if you like the idea of an office democracy, this device is ideal.) Below right, the striking leather and chrome desk of advertising agency Nadler & Larimer's chairman, Arch Nadler, is the focal point of his strong, modern office.

Not every office has to have a desk. Edward E. Elson, the president of Elson's and Atlanta News Agency, designed this stainless-steel-paneled room without one. In its stead, he uses the white marble cube and the octagonal art deco telephone table. Collecting is a hobby of Mr. Elson's, and the office enhances some of his most prized pieces: in the glass-enclosed cabinets are vases by Primavera, brass and steel figures by K. Hagenauer, bookends by Chase, a Lalique decanter, and a Muller Frères flask. The marble cube sits on an eighteenth-century Chinese rug and is surrounded by six Le Corbusier club chairs and a Le Corbusier pony-skin lounge chair. True to his individualistic spirit, Mr. Elson has defied tradition and made his office a personal living room.

Strong and masculine may not be words one associates with Louis Quinze and Rococo, but both fit this superb antique tulip wood writing table from the French firm of Didier Aaron. Ormolu—the gold leaf fused onto brass that decorates the desk here—was originated during the eighteenth century to protect vulnerable corners and hold veneer in place. The table is from the Russian Imperial Collection.

If the idea of a square desk
intrigues you, consider this
table by Brickel, with black
enameled steel pedestal
base and three-quarter-
inch marble top. The table
was designed in 1964 by
Ward Bennett, whose work
is noted for its purity of
form. In its design, the base
replicates a standard I-
beam used in building construction but here the lines
are softened to lend the
table a subtle, timeless
grace. The price is approximately $1500.

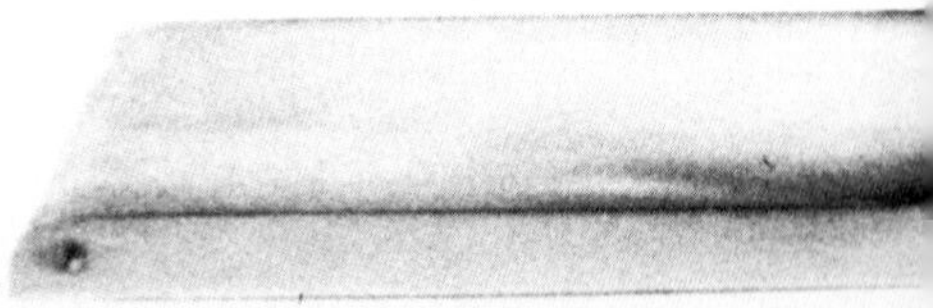

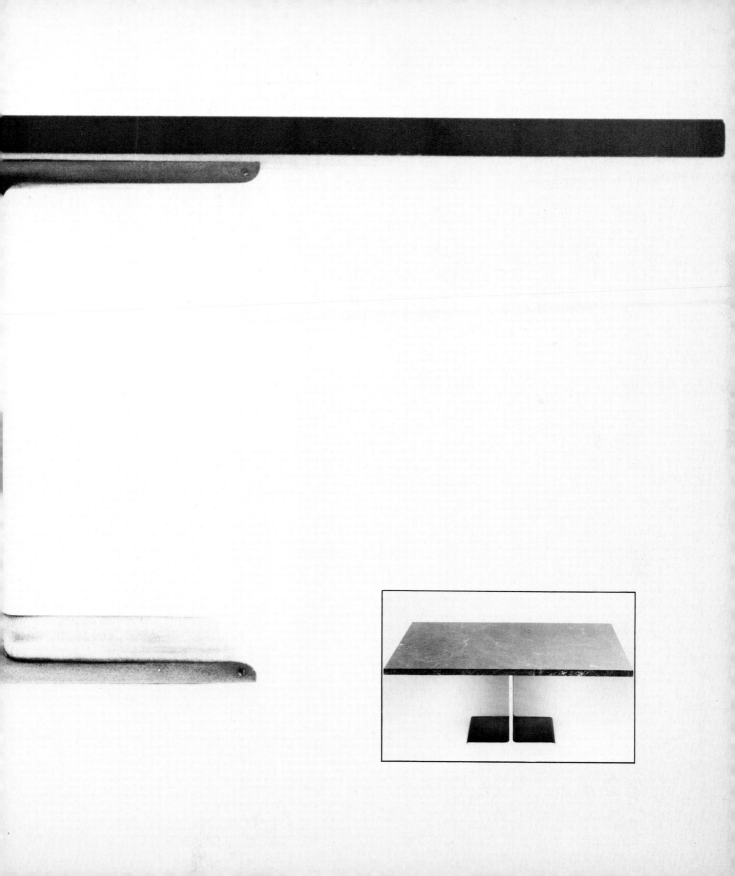

From Stair & Company, above, a beautifully grained and shaded mahogany English Chippendale double-sided writing table, c. 1760. The fret brackets are brass. Approximately $26,000. Compare it with the modern desk with granite top and leather base, by Dunbar, at right, which conveys an equivalent degree of style and solidity. The Dunbar desk, designed by de Polo/Dunbar, is also available with pedestals or with return; its top may be of marble or leather instead of granite, or the desk may be ordered entirely in oak or leather.

At the Hôtel du Collectionneur of the Arts Décoratifs
exhibition held in Paris in
1925, when Europe still
was recovering from World
War I, the critics disap-
proved of the inappro-
priately luxurious creations
of Jacques Emile Ruhl-
mann, who favored rare
woods and ivory. Ruhlmann
explained that he cared to
design only for the very
rich. The tapering reeded
leg merging into the body is
his invention; the art deco
desk shown here is of rosewood veneer with ivory handles and is available from
Didier Aaron for nearly
$50,000.

The original of this desk is in the Governor's Room of New York City's City Hall. It was used by George Washington from April 1789 to August 1790, when New York was the capital of the United States and City Hall was Federal Hall. Identical in appearance front and back, with simulated drawers on three sides, the desk was an American adaptation of a Sheraton design. Kittinger, established in Buffalo in 1866, is a major designer of reproduction furniture, and its precise copies combine good materials and hand finishing.

Above is an ash table-desk of recent design from Atelier International; it is available with or without the leather writing insert. At top right is a trestle table of fumed quarter-sawn white oak made by Leopold and J. George Stickley in New York around 1910 and available at the Jordan-Volpe gallery. The Stickleys' motto, stamped on their furniture, is a medieval boast borrowed from Jan van Eyck: *Als Il Kan* (All I Can). This style of design—Mission Oak—still is afford-able, although recently it has grown in popularity with collectors. It was a major part of the Arts and Crafts movement in Ameri-can furniture and it made the transition from period furniture to modern. The Stickley library table-desk, c. 1905, at bottom right, also available from Jordan-Volpe, is of mahogany with hand-hammered cop-per pulls on the three drawers.

This Adams desk, above, is English, called a "Partners Table" because it is the same on both sides and can be used by two people. This rare writing table, double-sided with an additional pull-out writing surface, has all the appeal of a gentler age. The color is a golden hue of faded and patined mahogany. Around $18,000 from Hyde Park Antiques, N.Y. Right is a desk designed in 1929 by Le Corbusier, available from Atelier International, and still as up-to-date as tomorrow. The base is of welded oval air-craft-type steel tubing, ground smooth and highly polished. Each desk is signed and numbered and available with either wood or glass top.

Above, a reproduction of a
Hepplewhite writing table of
very graceful proportions.
Made of mahogany in the
New York workshops of
Smith & Watson, it costs
approximately $3100.

Another reproduction, this of a Chippendale writing table made in England by Wood & Hogan. Similar in feeling, Chippendale and Hepplewhite can be distinguished by the Chinese motifs found only in Chippendale.

This self-proclaimed (and handsome) "executive desk in the female gender" by Vladimir Kagan features a top drawer that contains a lighted vanity with a flip-up mirror and a bottom drawer fitted to accommodate a telephone communications system and dictating equipment. Under the roll top is a Tiffany clock and a speaker phone with a polished chrome-plated letter paper and pen compartment. The desk is made to measure for its occupant.

This desk-table was designed in 1968 by Ward Bennett for the home of Fiat chairman Gianni Agnelli. The top is of seamless leather with bullnose (completely rounded) edge; the base is of polished plated steel. The desk, by Brickel, is available in custom sizes and, if desired, with drawers. The price is approximately $2500.

A Louis Seize mahogany traveling desk made by David Roentgen, one of the most prestigious German designers of the eighteenth century, who was an international influence. Roentgen is known for the beautiful marquetry of his pieces, for the architectural quality of his designs, and for their extraordinary construction. This piece, c. 1790, bears the arms of the Russian Imperial Court and is shown here from many angles, with all the compartments displayed and concealed. It can be yours for a mere $150,000 from Didier Aaron.

CHAIRS

Unless you spend most of your time at the golf club, the first thing to look for in a desk chair is comfort. Trying to work well in an uncomfortable chair is like wearing tight shoes on a grand tour of Europe. But there's no reason nowadays not to have both comfort and style.

The perfect desk chair is one that doesn't disappear behind your desk but doesn't dominate the desk —or you—either. Those very high-backed executive chairs that used to be popular tend to dwarf a person and make him or her look silly, like a judge in the wrong courtroom. For a well-put-together look, the chairs in front of the desk should be of the same design as the ones behind it —not necessarily identical, but perhaps the same chair without arms, or in a slightly scaled-down version. Chairs or sofas elsewhere in the room need only not clash with those at the desk; variation and contrast give an office interest and style. As for color, generally go easy— bright colors and busy patterns tend to be distracting. Neutral, or at least muted, colors in fabrics of interesting texture make most executives happiest. An antique adds beauty, a sense of permanence, and a touch of your personality.

But antiques and upholstery bring us to another subject—upkeep. Few offices are blessed with a decent cleaning service. If you're one of the many executives who must make do with a quick emptying of the ashtrays and swipe of the dustcloth, think hard before you upholster in white velvet or purchase an antique that requires loving hand-polishing to look its best. Fortunately, the variety in easy-to-care-for fabrics and finishes now is as vast as the selection of chairs and sofas that can make your office a place where both you and your visitors want to spend time.

If any office proves that good taste is timeless, it's that of David Rockefeller, chairman of the Chase Manhattan Bank. Designed in 1961, the room has remained precisely the same ever since. The comfortable keynote of Mr. Rockefeller's office is its variety of working and seating areas. All the chairs in this office are simple, functional, and upholstered in neutral shades. Note the chairs surrounding the conference table, shown in detail above. Designed by Ward Bennett for Lehigh-Leopold, and upholstered in tan leather, these are swivel chairs, only occasionally used for conferences. Like the other chairs and the sofa, they make no statement of their own but serve as a backdrop for the featured attraction of the office, the fabled art collection—paintings by Picasso, Matisse, Corot, superb examples of ancient and modern sculpture, and *objets*. Yet the large room accommodates its grandeur without being intimidating or showy. For all its magnificence, the art augments Mr. Rockefeller's taste rather than overshadowing him.

At left, the side chairs and sofa, designed by Granick, are upholstered in natural South American wool. The way Mr. Rockefeller maintains the light colors of upholstery and carpeting is simple—they are reupholstered when they are soiled. From every angle, the art is enhanced by its placement. At the end of the passageway hangs a celebrated Rothko; the twelfth-century wooden Jizo figure stands guard.

Even in Mr. Rockefeller's private bathroom, art lends its glow. On the marble counter sits a Willi Gutman metal sculpture.

If one had to guess who concocted this flamboyantly sensual art deco fantasy, first choice would likely be fashion designer and entrepreneur Diane Von Furstenberg. She asked her designer for a mixture of transatlantic ocean liner and Esther Williams movie, and she got it. Perhaps the major element is the gray velvet art deco chairs—a blend of drop-dead elegance and sheer theater. But only a bigger-than-life person could get away with an office like this one—and with the visual laboratory above

the art nouveau desk. Art
deco, with its ornate Persian influences, its often
overwhelming abundance
of zigzags and Lucite, may
serve best in accent pieces
—a lamp, a pillow, an ashtray.

The office of Xerox president David T. Kearns is a room with more than one advantage. Its neutral colors and clean lines transmit a feeling of comfort and restraint; the pastoral painting is pleasing but not overpowering. The Stendig sofa and lounge chairs in the meeting area are more customarily found in reception rooms—chairs that invite one to lean back and relax. For Mr. Kearns, they're an informal alternative to the nearby desk–conference table work area.

The chairs surrounding Mr. Kearns's desk are by Helikon, their upholstery by Scalamandré. The window treatment is minimal, putting as little as possible between Mr. Kearns and the view.

The couch and chairs in the office of John Marion, president of Sotheby Parke Bernet, are central in creating the relaxed, homelike environment here—important when many of the visitors are tensely thinking about parting with valuable possessions or even their family homes to this premier auction house. The mahogany armchairs are Regency antiques. The art on Mr. Marion's walls changes with the company's inventory. Shown here, reading clockwise from left: Pierre Bonnard, *Woman in a Bathtub*, circa 1917; Pierre-Auguste Renoir, *The Loge*, 1897; Renoir, *Bather Drying Her Feet*, circa 1907.

Ahmet Ertegun is chairman of Atlantic Recording Corporation, and his Knoll chairs and side couches have held the derrieres of superstars like Mick Jagger and Led Zeppelin. The office, planned to convey the feeling of a sitting room because Mr. Ertegun entertains frequently here, also projects, with its classic Parsons desk and sleek wall units, an atmosphere of cozy efficiency. The bowl of orchids on the table adds, as flowers always do, a further touch of warmth.

Geraldine Stutz was running Henri Bendel, New York's chicest department store, when women were rare in executive suites; her office reflects her feminine brand of style and strength. The lavish use of contrasting fabrics and bright colors might be distracting in a less creative business—here it's electric. On the wall, an antique armoire opens to reveal a three-way mirror, designed by H. McKim Glazebrook, who also redesigned Bendel's main floor. The informal banquette, piled with pillows, is used weekly for large meetings. The rattan desk chair and the visitors' chairs are identical, suggesting equality. Rattan, normally too casual for executive use, works here. Ms. Stutz solves the problem of storage by using the round storage basket at her feet.

Here is your basic-black-and-chrome, get-down-to-business office—but with a big difference. Most executives like to make it clear who's in charge behind the desk and who's just visiting: Lee Berendt, president of Commodity Exchange, has chosen an oval table instead of a desk. Only the desk chair from Atelier International and the guest chairs from Krueger indicate that there are degrees of power here.

One-time Southerner Larry Nachman moved the New York offices of Swirl, a company that manufactures loungewear designed by Bill Tice and others, to Rockefeller Center because he wanted to be able to open his windows. With cross ventilation, aided by something you don't often see in an office—a ceiling fan—he's able to do without air conditioning. The desk chair, English, circa 1840, reupholstered in leather, comes from New Orleans, the town where Mr. Nachman went to college. Along with the plush velvet upholstery of the Knoll guest chairs, and the fan, it makes him feel right back at home.

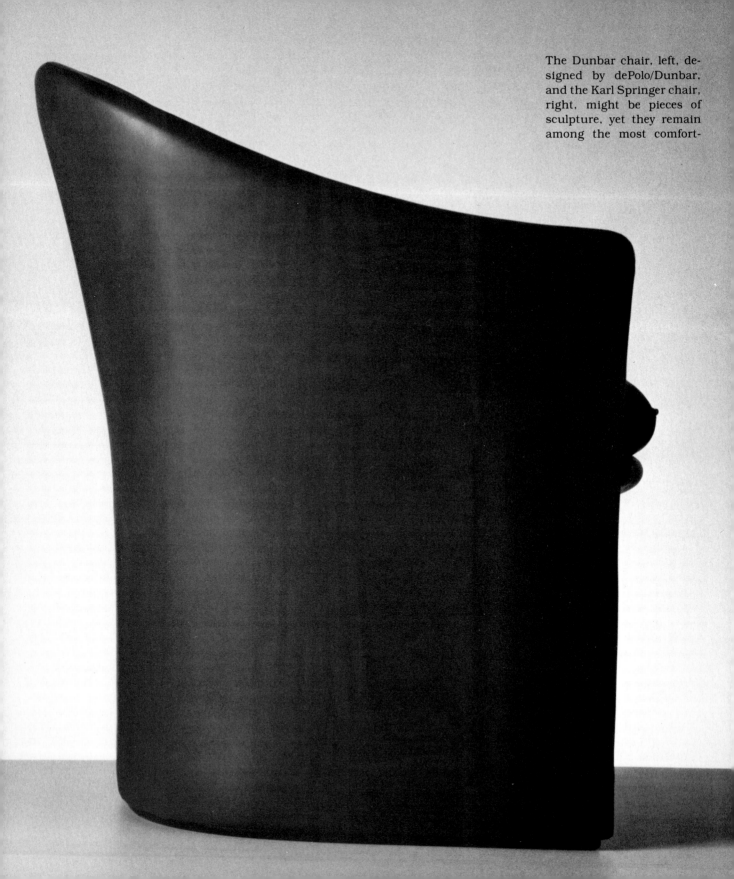

The Dunbar chair, left, designed by dePolo/Dunbar, and the Karl Springer chair, right, might be pieces of sculpture, yet they remain among the most comfortable available. Both chairs could function beautifully as guest or conference chairs; the Dunbar serves excellently behind a desk as well.

The chair below, of black Claro leather, was designed by Le Corbusier in 1929 and quickly became a classic. How effectively it can be used is demonstrated in Edward Elson's office (pages 28 and 29).

Above, an armchair by Knoll in nickel-finish steel, upholstered in handwoven wool. It won't fit in everywhere, but wherever it's found, it will be a conversation piece. Below, Knoll's Brno chair, designed by Mies van der Rohe. This classic often is imitated, but rarely with much success. The frame here is polished stainless steel.

Two chairs that shine with good design. Above, a Knoll armchair by William Stephens. The gracefulness of the chair's arms, thin laminations of wood veneer, separates it from its many less-expensive imitations. Below, a Knoll swivel-tilt desk chair by Andrew Ivar Morrison and Bruce R. Hannah. The frame and base are of cast aluminum.

The classic Ward Bennett side chair from Brickel. The pull-up chair with its low arms and continuous carved wood frame, upholstered here in leather, is ideal for a conference, guest, or dining chair. It costs about $1100, plus fabric.

Armchair with round carved wood frame of oiled natural ash, knife-edge seat cushion, caned seat and back. Ward Bennett for Brickel, at approximately $1100, plus fabric.

Both chairs above by Ward Bennett. Above left, the Mobius Executive armchair is fully upholstered, with low back and carved wood frame, suitable for use at a desk. Above right, a more casual upholstered armchair for use at conference or dining table. Right is Knoll's small swivel armchair designed by Max Pearson. The base is stainless steel with adjustable swivel and tilt mechanism, upholstery of foam rubber over molded plastic shells. Approximate costs are $1600, $1100, and $800 respectively, plus fabric.

At left, the Barbar Management chair from Atelier International—comfortable, serious, yet still conceived and executed beautifully. At right, an armchair designed by Ben Baldwin of Jack Lenor Larsen, originally for the Ritz Carlton Bar in Boston. The frame is solid maple.

Nicos Zographos is an internationally noted architectural, interior, and furniture designer. His chairs—all of them pieces of art as well as places to sit; his criteria—form and definition and that elusive concern for the human body. The chair shown here comes fully upholstered in fabric or leather.

The chair above, shown in leather, has a base of mirror-polished stainless steel; it also is available in bronze.

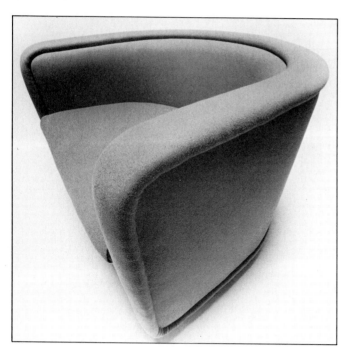

The Brickel U-Chair, shown in two versions, was designed by Ward Bennett in 1977, specifically for the changing, smaller proportions of today's offices. Within small spaces, functional forms usually seem austere and ineffective, taking from an interior rather than adding to it. With a creative sense of design and a rational approach, Bennett designed this chair to fill the gap. The chair is casual and light in scale, and the seamless upholstery gives it a rich look, ideal for reception areas as well as for offices.

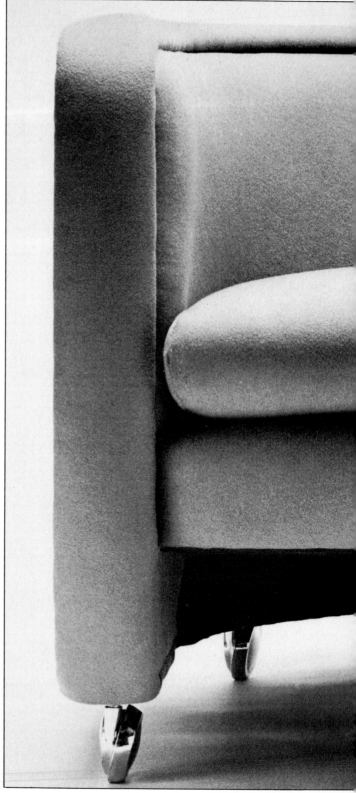

Above, the companion U-Settee, designed by Ward Bennett, is shown here upholstered in a reversible natural-fiber 100-percent Irish tweed, also designed by Mr. Bennett. Each color consists of four to six color fibers. Approximately $1850, plus fabric. Left, Mr. Bennett's Cartouche sofa.

The cartouche was an oval symbol embossed on the possessions of the royal family in ancient Egypt. Whether Mr. Bennett named the sofa to make reference to the shape of the sofa or to the sort of people who can afford to sit in it is hard to say. Approximately $3450, plus fabric.

An extremely rare Queen Anne corner chair, c. 1740, with a highly unusual extra back. This chair, made in Rhode Island, still has the original upholstery on the seat. There are only about six other existing examples of this chair, two in the Henry Francis Dupont Winterthur Museum in Delaware. From Bernard & S. Dean Levy, costing approximately $28,500.

An English George III mahogany exercise chair, or "Chamber Horse," used in the second half of the eighteenth century, from Florian Papp. Originally the seat cushion harbored a set of springs that worked like a bellows, yielding under the weight of a healthy posterior, then pushing back up again as the sitter, with the aid of his arms, sought his rather modest regimen.

Top left, Knoll's classic Pollock chair, a swivel armchair that's one of the most popular desk chairs around —and with reason: This is a sturdy office chair, also suitable as a conference room or guest chair, that's sensibly priced and never seems to go out of style. The base is stainless steel over steel armature, and the chair, with an adjustable swivel and tilt mechanism, is available in a variety of finishes. Top right is one of the Thonet versions of Mies van der Rohe's 1930 chair; the base here is of sleek, polished, chrome-plated tubular steel. It is one of the few less-expensive versions of the Brno chair that is well-executed and of good value. $270, plus fabric. Bottom right, an unusual country yew wood spindle-back Windsor armchair from Florian Papp. The seat is inlaid in a compass motif, four quadrants of 90 degrees centering a bird. Legs are splayed and bobbin-turned. Flemish, c. 1800.

One of a set of six Chinese red lacquered side chairs, made in China around 1810. Models of superb decoration and splendid proportion, they are hand carved as well as hand painted. $23,000 for the six, from The Incurable Collector.

TABLES

Unlike desks, tables allow the executive a wide range of expression. Desks almost always are rectangular. Tables can be virtually any shape the imagination can come up with: Consider, for example, Philip Johnson's triangular fantasy for General American Life's conference room (on pages 102 and 103). In dining rooms especially, executives and designers become almost playful. Bob Fomon's office at E. F. Hutton is reasonably sober; yet in the Hutton dining room (pages 114 and 115) the table is of pink granite. There are a number of reasons for this freedom: Conference rooms and dining rooms are group rooms that don't require "power positions." And the table in a conference room or dining room almost always is the only major shape—it doesn't have to go with anything or play second fiddle. Not so in the office itself, where it's important to make sure the table complements the desk and doesn't fight with it. But even there a wide range of shapes is possible, and one superb small table can be an island of style in an otherwise standardized office.

If advertising agencies ate their accounts' products, the fare here would include McDonald's hamburgers, Campbell's Soup, Bisquick, and Tuna Helper, with Anheuser-Busch beer for refreshments. Presumably the luncheons in the dining room of Needham, Harper & Steers are more formal.

Planned as the private dining room–conference room of agency chairman Paul Harper, the room is booked constantly by other senior executives when Mr. Harper isn't using it. And no wonder. The pedestal table and chairs are by Zographos and balance intimacy with efficiency.

Even in the office proper, Mr. Harper favors a table-desk—and an uncluttered one. A chief executive officer spends more time with people than with papers. The table-desk here is a custom design by ISD, as are the leather-wrapped storage cube and the corner cube-table.

The office of Katharine Graham, chairman of The Washington Post Company, was designed to her specifications; an informal seating area was a high priority. Above, that area, as photographed from her desk; the sofa and lounge chairs are by Knoll, the guest chairs by ICF, upholstered in taupe suede. At right, the adjoining private dining room—conference room carries out the brisk, cheerful feeling. Like Mrs. Graham's office, it is a relaxed and friendly but businesslike room. The table, custom made by Lehigh-Leopold, has an opaque lacquer top; the chairs are by Knoll, upholstered in wool. An executive dining room need not be, and often is not, forbidding or imposing. Guests can, and should, make the room.

Anspach Grossman Portugal is in the design business, creating corporate identities, including logos —Citibank's is theirs, and so are AMF and Continental Group Ltd. Not surprisingly, Gene Grossman's office is clearly elegant, a perfect blending of a few fine elements. The Apollo leather-topped table serves as desk and conference table; Mr. Grossman also uses his drawing board as a desk. The executive chair is the Knoll classic Pollock chair; the three guest chairs are by Mies van der Rohe. The single ficus tree adds warmth and color to the room.

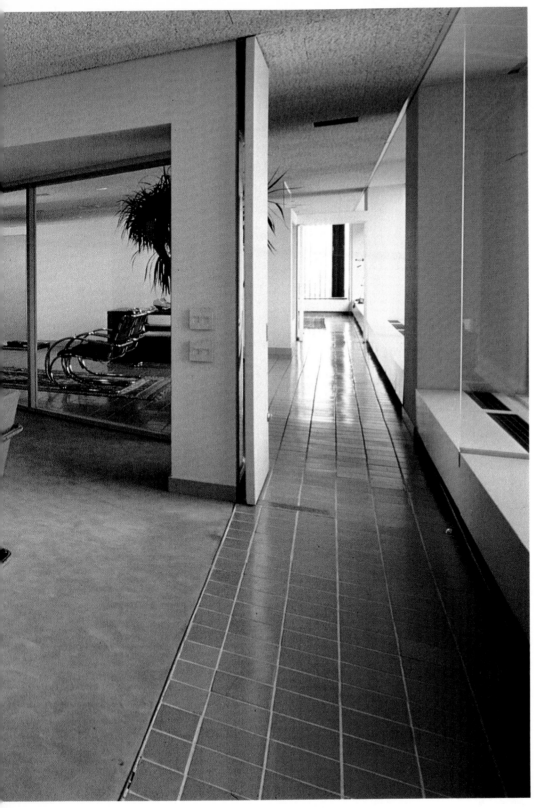

Interconnect Planning Corporation manufactures telephone systems of the future. Its conference area keys into that image with minimal elements, all of them functioning optimally. The chairs are burgundy-covered Knoll Brno chairs. The table of Russo Verde marble seems to grow from the cut-velvet carpet. Though expensive, marble conveys the feeling of luxury and permanence as few materials do; it is especially effective in a conference room.

The triangular building that headquarters General American Life Insurance Company, the largest life insurance company in Missouri, was designed by Philip Johnson (the Museum of Modern Art in New York and the Pennzoil Building in Houston are among his other achievements). Mr. Johnson also oversaw the interior furnishing of the offices. The echoing triangular table in the conference room is of three-inch-thick granite from Italy, its base of brass. The walls are covered in brown Ultrasuede.

103

The boardroom of the Banco di Roma is a study in luxury—an Italian red Lavanto marble table that rests on a steel base, leather chairs by Zographos. The custom-loomed carpet carries out the design of the diamond-shaped columns on the exterior of the building.

Another conference room, another bank, another table—but again an aura of permanence and substance: The boardroom of the First Atlanta Corporation gives one the sense that the institution and its members have been here for a long time and will be here for a long time to come. When the bank holding company, founded in 1865, moved in 1969 from its original building, the boardroom was painstakingly reconstructed, piece by piece; the bank built an exact replica. The wood paneling is pecan, bleached to the color in the original boardroom. The Oriental rug removes the institutional feeling of any office and creates a beauty of its own.

Three of the dining rooms at the J. Henry Schroder Bank in New York are referred to by Chairman Mark Maged as the Green Room, the Gray Room, and the Red Room. The differing color schemes, table shapes, furnishings, and art create three strikingly different environments. The Gray Room, near right, centers on a dining table made of burl wood. On the walls are prints by Dieter Roth and Joseph Albers.

The table in the Green Room, above, is of Verde Acceglio marble, custom-designed by Ferguson Sorrentino. Chagall lithographs animate the room. The Red Room's tulip table and chairs were designed by Eero Saarinen. The art in the dining rooms, as throughout the bank, was chosen carefully, not ordered indiscriminately to match the decor, an unfortunate tendency of many corporations. The china used in all the dining rooms is made by Royal Worcester and incorporates the Schroder family crest.

Again, an office doesn't have to be large to be well designed. Golo Footwear Corporation, like many manufacturing companies, must devote most of its space to its showroom selling area, and so individual offices tend to be small. In the office of president Arthur Samuels, Jr., the horseshoe-shaped desk was custom designed to serve two functions, as conference table and desk. The desk is of practical, easy-care Formica laminate. Surrounding the desk are the famous Pollock chairs from Knoll.

111

Some boardroom tables have invisible built-in speakers. In this boardroom the speakers seem to add to the power of the place.

One would hate to come un-
prepared to a meeting in so
awesome a room, the boardroom of Crocker National
Bank in Los Angeles. Much
of the room's effect comes
from the richness of the
materials. The U-shaped
table, which seats 28, was
designed by Bert England,
and is of highly polished
bartiki wood. The stripe of
light on the rug leads like a
red carpet to the seat of
power in the room. In the
reception area, above, the
custom-designed reception
desk incorporates a well-
integrated communications
and security system.

Outside the unadorned window, the city seems to be a toy for international financiers to play with. Inside, the Gardner Lever granite table and Lever stainless steel and leather chairs lend the dining rooms at E. F. Hutton a modern and international look that reinforces the company's image.

The conference table at left, designed for Sunar by Douglas Ball, has a top of imported Verde Antique marble, one and one-half inches thick, with a bull-nose edge. The base is steel in a matte-black finish.

The Thonet table above has a tubular chrome base with self-leveling glides and a self-edged plastic laminate top. Its modest price—$240 —makes it an excellent example of first-rate design at a reasonable cost.

The Kyoto coffee table from
Sunar is made of beech-
wood with rosewood inlay.
The criss-cross pattern is
reminiscent of a Japanese
temple. The price is approximately $5000.

Karl Springer's tables are rich and glossy objects that almost always stand out even in a crowd of fine furniture. This table, made of parchment, dried and lacquered, would be splendid in a dining room or even a conference room.

At left, the Knoll dining table designed by Eero Saarinen. Shown here with a Madera marble top and a white fused-finish pedestal, the table is available in a variety of colors and finishes. From $2200 to $3500.

Above, the materials are strikingly combined in this mahogany table with polished chrome legs, designed by Charles Pfister, from Knoll.

Castelli's LC table, shown here with dark walnut top and tubular chrome base, was designed to be "the focal point of a room." Castelli's parent company, Anonima Castelli, was started in Italy in the latter part of the nineteenth century as an artisan workshop. Castelli Furniture came to the United States in 1974. Italy's emergence during the last decade as the dominant force in consumer products design has already been seen in the work of every other European country and now is having its effect in the United States.

Cini Boeri's Lunario table for Knoll makes a dramatically elegant statement. The glass top, available in a round or an oval, is cantilevered from a polished steel base, creating a striking juxtaposition of materials and forms. Approximately $2500.

The conference table, forty-eight inches in diameter and suitable also as a table-desk, has a graceful, mirror-polished stainless steel base. The bullnose-edged top of this table from Zographos is of marble, available in several shades.

The low coffee table, also from Zographos, is an item one might be tempted to steal from an office and take home. The top of this sculptural piece is of polished glass, the base of polished steel.

129

The La Basilica table from Atelier International is an up-to-date refectory table, designed by Mario Bellini, and made in a special natural Italian walnut with a variety of light-to-dark sapwood colorations. The cost is approximately $3800.

LIGHTING

It used to be, all you asked of the lights in your office was that they turn on. No longer! As today's executives realize, lighting shapes the look of an office more than a view, more even than furniture. The most expensive decor can lose all subtlety and depth under glaring illumination; the simplest office may acquire an elegance in soft chiaroscuro. For most offices, the less lighting the better, but choices are still as varied as, well, the spectrum.

Notice, for instance, the natural light of J. Howard Johnson's office (pages 140–141), the play of artificial light in the offices of the Williams Companies (pages 154–155), the neon sculpture in the screening room of George Barrie of Fabergé (page 137). Most senior executives prefer not to clutter their desks with lamps, and so most lighting is indirect—recessed incandescent ceiling lights provide the most unobtrusive illumination. However, hanging lights, when they're attractive, can be an important design element, and exposed track lighting, especially in a modern office, can add to the room's appeal. The only kind of lighting to avoid is fluorescent. No matter how muted or recessed it is, fluorescent light shrieks of mass production, is dreadful to work by, and makes both the room and the people in it look ghastly. If you have fluorescent lights, turn them off and use lamps instead. Natural lighting is a big bonus—it's the airiest and most restful light. For that reason, window treatments should be kept simple: neutral, vertical blinds, slim horizontal blinds, or light curtains make the most of natural light. If the windows open onto a view, don't feel compelled to cover it up.

Fabergé is a cosmetics company with brands "Babe" and "Brut" and its eye on the future. The office of Chairman George Barrie uses dramatic spotlighting to throw into relief the exciting architectural lines and modular furniture that emphasize the company's theme.

Above, the bathroom, which carries out the space-age design of Mr. Barrie's office suite. The door closes with the push of a button. At right, a neon sculpture is found in the screening room where commercials are previewed.

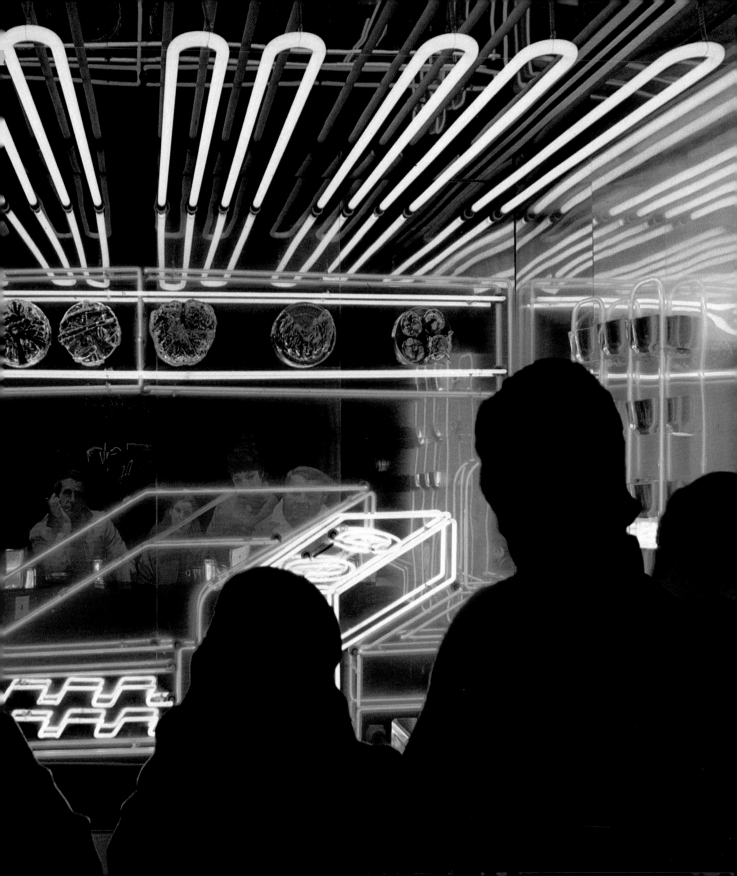

When the Bank of Tokyo acquired the Southern California First National Bank of San Diego to become California First Bank, the international and commercial strengths of the Japanese institution melded with the retail banking acumen of the American. In the office of Masao Tsuyama, chairman of the board of the California First Bank, East meets West once more. The use of venetian blinds as a divider between Mr. Tsuyama's office and those of the bank's senior officers creates a play of light within and without that transforms the room itself into a sculpture of sunshine and shadow.

Above, a granite-top table by Cedric Hartman reflects some of the sparkle.

Washed by sunlight, the office of J. Howard Johnson, president of the Unitrex Division of Merchants Corporation of America, combines ornate architectural detail with the best of modern design. The blues, beiges, and tomato reds animate the paneled walls and plasterwork ceiling in this Fifth Avenue penthouse office. The ceiling, invisible in most offices, here is almost a centerpiece. Notice how meticulously the recessed lighting has been integrated into the plasterwork design.

A carefully achieved marriage of natural and artificial lighting makes the dining room of IBM's Management Development Center a pleasant place in which to lunch. The natural wood of the chairs and the stone walls contribute to creating a country ambience beneath sleek contemporary chandeliers.

Founded in 1896, Sperry and Hutchinson is the parent company to one of the largest furnishings manufacturing groups in the country. The intimacy of the meeting area in the office of Chairman James T. Mills is enhanced by the softly diffused light cast by two handsome porcelain lamps. The hue of the petaled lamp bases picks up the color of the coffee table, constructed of wood covered with linen and lacquered. The walls, sofa, and two love seats are covered in a slubbed wool; the Oriental rug repeats the colors of the handwoven wall hanging, creating the illusion that the two are one continuous, harmonious element. It is the lighting, varied rather than constant, that animates and accentuates the warm textures in this room.

Designed by Tom John (better known for Broadway, movie, and television sets, which include *The Wiz*, *Sybil*, *Taxi*, and *Good Morning, America*), the dramatically lighted entrance hall to the office of Warner Bros. chairman Ted Ashley prepares the visitor for the glamour within. The silver-plated doors once graced a downtown Los Angeles art deco skyscraper. The copper borders were added to extend the doors' size. Above, in Mr. Ashley's office, sunlight streams in through windows rescued from the set of a film entitled *Hotel* and installed here in place of a blank wall. Mr. Ashley's desk, made in Paris, is of stainless steel with a glass base, reversing the usual pattern.

Illuminating an impressive collection of art deco furnishings and *objets* in Ted Ashley's office is a dazzling three-tiered lighting fixture. The art deco brass cabinet on the wall, right, is from the Newell Galleries; the mirror on the wall, left, was made from two art deco headboards, also from Newell, and the art deco wall fixtures come from South America. The two original art deco chairs are covered in red mohair, making a splash of color in what is otherwise a subdued room, with its gray-flannel-covered walls. Art deco seems almost made to order for the office of a modern-day Hollywood mogul, yet the room, for all its flash, shows taste and restraint.

Left, the elevator lobby of the National Bank of Tulsa is a symphony in light and shade, setting off to best advantage the sculpture by James Rosati.

Center and right, the dining room of the bank. Light, natural by day, artificial by night, is a dramatic element of design. The view is not obscured, but direct sunlight is filtered by the casement curtains of Scalamandré wool. The ceiling light fixture was designed by Edison Price, Inc.

The entire reception area and stair hall of Wender, Murase & White, a New York City law firm, was designed so that natural light would penetrate through to the offices. Artificial lighting enhances and extends the natural light; the wall-mounted fixtures are an integral part of the American elm paneling. The fixtures are made of concentric spun aluminum rings; a quartz light within washes the ceiling with an even intensity.

The Williams Companies, an energy conglomerate in Tulsa, Oklahoma, has knock-out-your-eye architecture, design, furnishings, and what has to be called "special effects." Left, a detail of the brass balcony railing on the stairway between floors is illuminated by the constantly changing light from the skylight above. The flooring is Verde Acceglio and Saint Florient Rose marbles. Above, the reception garden houses the fountain pool. The sound of gently splashing water and a view of the Tulsa skyline create a tranquil oasis.

Here's an office that's as big as all New York. Ronald Saypol, president of the Lionel Corporation, sits almost literally on top of the world. The muted colors are soothing and form a natural backdrop to the unadorned, unparalleled view. Light glints off the glass-block wall onto the two-tone parchment desk by Karl Springer. The two-level taupe carpeting is from Patterson, Flynn & Martin. The use of plants enhances the suspended-in-the-sky feeling of the room.

156

This conference room, with its glass-block walls, floats like a jeweled island in the center of the Lionel space. The use of glass here to increase clarity and light creates a lofty, airy feeling, but manages not to get in the way of business.

The Barbinis have been glass blowers on Murano, the isle of glassmakers, near Venice, since the seventeenth century. The lamp here and several others shown on the following two pages were done by the Barbini family in collabo-

ration with Lighting Associates. They blend creative
Italian design, the most exciting in the field today,
with functional American
technology. Above, a hanging lamp 22 inches in di-
ameter, saline-etched with
a burgundy top and border.

A table lamp by Barbini for Lighting Associates, of hand-blown, saline-etched glass. The shade, which is removable, is of varied thicknesses of white and clear glass; the base is gray-black.

The Taccia table lamp, from Atelier International, has a white-enameled spun-aluminum concave reflector resting on a clear glass bowl. The top tilts easily, making the lamp useful also as a spotlight. Available with a black or natural aluminum base.

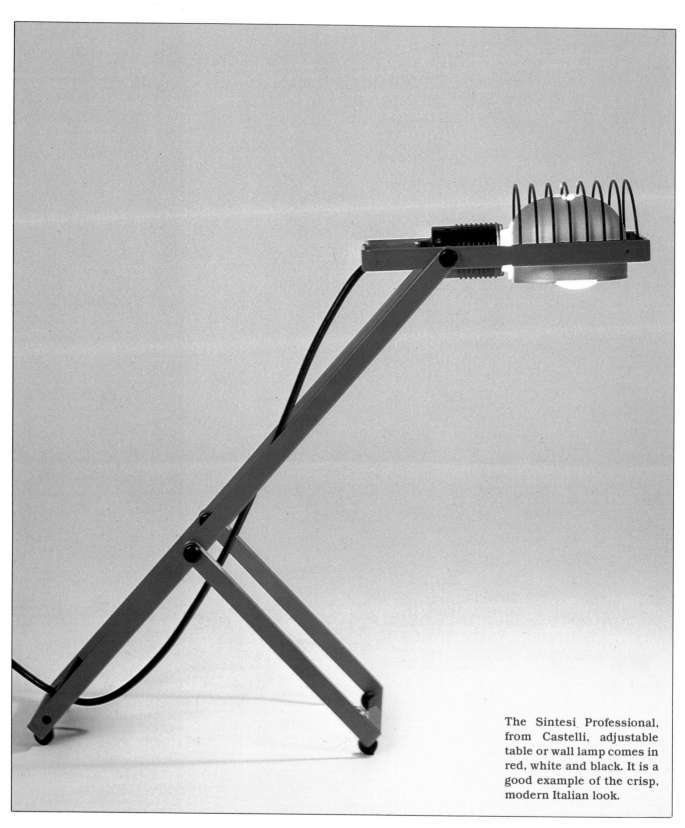

The Sintesi Professional, from Castelli, adjustable table or wall lamp comes in red, white and black. It is a good example of the crisp, modern Italian look.

Made of glass, in colors of amber or rose quartz, this lamp by Barbini looks more like a piece of sculpture as the soft light is suffused through the glass.

ACCESSORIES

Accessories are extras, and to puritan minds, that might make them seem out of place—if not downright distracting—in an executive's office. But accessories can also provide an extra touch of style that transforms an office of mere furniture into a quiet fashion statement. They also announce that whatever role a designer may have played in assembling that furniture, *you* had the taste and panache to make the office your own. Of course, you can also trumpet your lack of taste with pictures of your family (too intimate for an office), awards and diplomas (the best people, we've found in our tour of hundreds of offices, display the fewest), and desk sets and pen and pencil sets (they look pretentious). The major thing to avoid is clutter. Tables and desks ought to be clean and neat and ready for work. Nothing undermines authority more than a mess of last week's memos. Pens and pencils should be in a drawer and not on the desk (unless you have a single, striking pencil holder). Ashtrays should be small and inconspicuous, designed for practicality, not for artistic display. Keep your calculator in a drawer, too; even a telephone ideally should be put out of sight, installed below or on the side of the desk. The few objects on your desk should show your taste, style, and personality—as do the objects in this section, from the sterling silver Georgian skewer used as a letter opener, to the tiny tortoise-shell desk clock. Accessories follow you out of the office as well. Your attaché case, your pen, or your diary can often say as much about you as your clothes.

The offices of Malcolm S. Forbes, publisher of *Forbes* Magazine, might be in a London townhouse, the appointments in a museum. Indeed, this room was designed by architect Thomas Hastings, whose credits include the Frick Museum and the New York Public Library. On the desk are several fine examples of the gold and enamel art of Peter Carl Fabergé, the Russian court jeweler.

The wine cellar, noted for its selection of Premier Cru Lafite Rothschild, marries a sixteenth-century Italian refectory table to twentieth-century Italian Plexiglas chairs. The silver stag-head stirrup cups decorating the beams are from Tiffany and are engraved to commemorate lunches held for leaders of industry and finance. The grilled door, from a Spanish monastery, hides a small pantry. The cellar is occasionally used for corporate luncheons.

The dining room was designed as a setting for two outstanding jewels of Mr. Forbes's collection of *objets:* the nineteenth-century hand-painted Bavarian china and the silver-gilt flatware by Fabergé. The painting is by the late American realist Edward Melcarth.

Halston, the designer, uses the drama of a spectacular view and a spectacular color to create a striking yet elegant office.

The red lacquered table in Halston's office and matching telephone cube were designed by Charles Pfister. In the small photograph, above, a still life of accessories by Halston's friend Elsa Peretti. A silver candlestick, a silver pen on a black nephrite base, and silver objects nestle beside the orchids. Outside the glass walls, the city becomes the ultimate accessory.

You would not know if you were not told that this is the shared conference area of the two senior partners of the law firm Bracewell & Patterson of Houston, Texas. The natural light pouring in through the windows illuminates a superb Dhurrie rug. The telescope emphasizes the unusual and arresting shape of the room, located in the triangular Pennzoil building. Above, the office of partner Searcy Bracewell shows that Early American furniture and accessories can be completely at ease in a modern setting.

Ebony and *Jet* magazines are among the numerous enterprises of John H. Johnson, publisher. A few carefully selected objects highlighted by examples of African art grace this massively proportioned office.

Mr. Johnson's exercise room—complete with barber chair and massage and weight-lifting equipment—an enviable accessory.

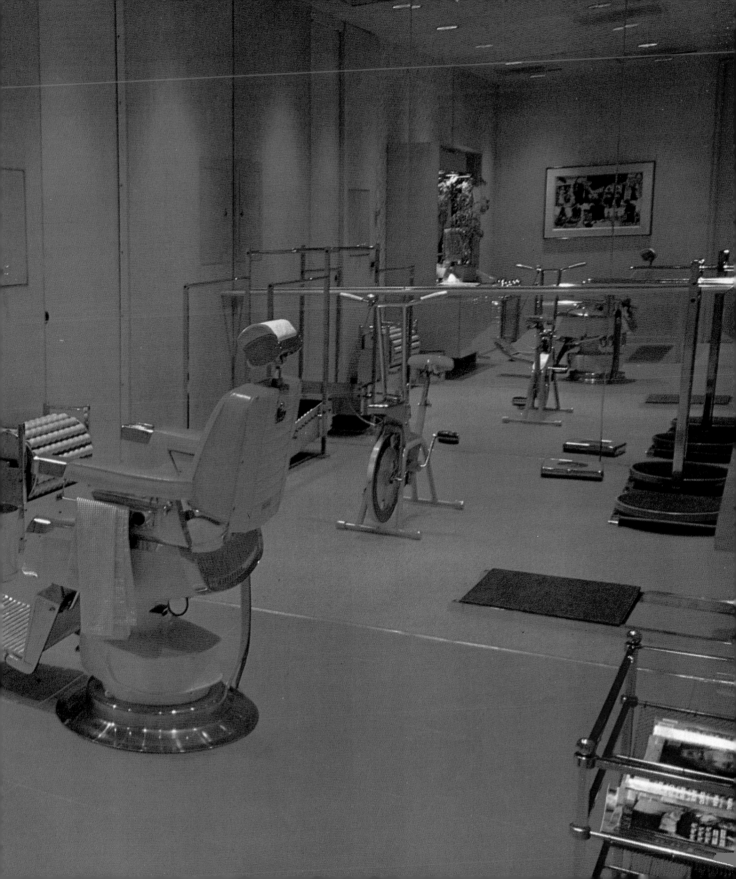

The office of Edward Lee Cave, chairman of the real estate division of Sotheby Parke Bernet, is a rich room —in furnishings, in color, in feeling. Yet it remains comfortable and inviting. The furniture is a faultless combination of antiques and comfortable contemporary pieces. The desk is a Chinese hardwood table, c. 1820, its rectangular top and frieze carved with strapwork, mounted on open fretwork legs. The George III mahogany sideboard is late eighteenth century. The side chairs are Edwardian and the glass-and-tea-paper coffee table is art deco. Art dominates this room: Above the sofa hangs a fine Chinese export—a reverse painting on glass from the early 19th century.

The desk of Oppenheimer & Co. chairman Jack Nash is like the bow of a ship. The accessories in this room at the helm of a major brokerage firm are in fact futuristic electronic devices. The office centers on Mr. Nash's command post, from which he can consult, even during meetings, the stock ticker tape recessed in the wall. The leather sofas are from Atelier International, the desk chair from Herman Miller. The floor tile is by Furstenberg.

A senior corporate executive of Murjani, the $300-million-dollar company that markets Gloria Vanderbilt jeans, spends an estimated twelve to fifteen hours a day in his office. This bathroom, which includes a sauna, a massage table, and a shower, brings him more than the comforts of home.

Remington bronzes and Chinese ivories accent the office of Arthur Rubloff, the real estate developer credited with having created Chicago's Magnificent Mile, on North Michigan Avenue, and also with having designed his own office. The desk, of rosewood and marble, is nine and one-half feet long and five feet wide and so heavy that a steel frame had to be anchored into the rosewood floor to lend sufficient support. Accessories do not have to be priceless to be valuable: To the right of the desk is a brass spittoon purchased for Mr. Rubloff by his father.

In Mr. Rubloff's dining room, the crystal is Waterford, the china Royal Crown Derby, the flatware Pfeiffer Mangasil, the linen place mats and napkins handmade by Franklin Bayer. The glass-enclosed cabinet houses a paperweight collection, his second. He donated the first, estimated at a value of $4.5 million, to the Chicago Art Institute. Above, choice pieces of crystal rest on top of a hand-carved Oriental table.

An office as full of charm, humor, and hominess as you're likely ever to see— and on top of that, it's part of a cathedral. The Very Reverend James Parks Morton, Dean of the Cathedral of St. John the Divine in New York, uses with commendable panache and effect a late-sixteenth-century Spanish refectory table. The accessories are intensely personal, perhaps the most so, Dean Morton's collection of rocks, gathered in East Hampton and Colorado. This is an office that breaks every rule—and gets away with it.

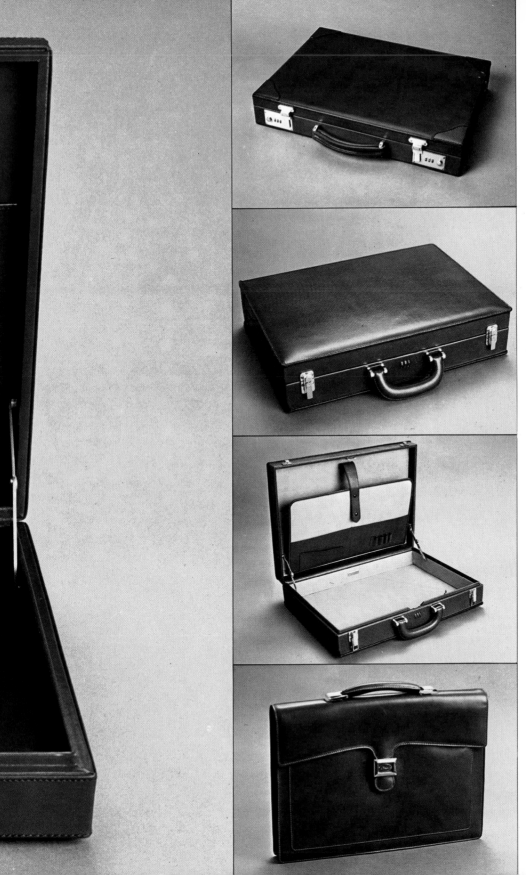

The most important accessory is the attaché case, and the most important color, dark brown or burgundy. Avoid an attaché case emblazoned with initials not your own—they're pretentious and project insecurity. The simplest shape is the best. Avoid a case with disappearing handles—the kind that collapse into the case. Such cases are neither "clutch" nor "professor," and make no clear statement. There are, by the way, no "female" attaché cases; a well-designed attaché case suits both genders equally well. Here and on the next two pages are some of the best examples.

At far left, the very slim English attaché case is made of tan calfskin and available at Alfred Dunhill of London. Approximately $525.

At left, top, a suede-lined briefcase with combination lock. Available at Mädler Park Avenue. Approximately $650.

Second and third from top, shown closed and open, the Bottega Veneta combination-lock pressed-calf attaché case is priced under $375 and has a legal-size file system.

At bottom, a trim, professor-type attaché case in rich teak from Gucci. Approximately $650.

195

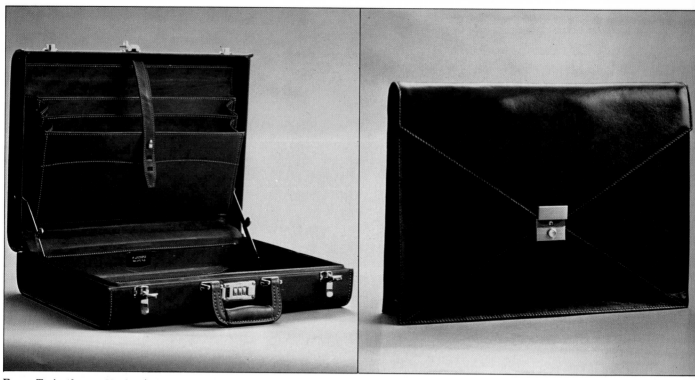

From T. Anthony. Under $450.

This leather folio by Lancel costs under $150.

From Bottega Veneta, a "Limited Edition Folio."
Approximately $550.

A pressed-calf portfolio from Bottega Veneta, shown open
and closed. Approximately $300.

Classic Mark Cross. Under $600.

From Mädler Park Avenue, a "professor" attaché. Approximately $650.

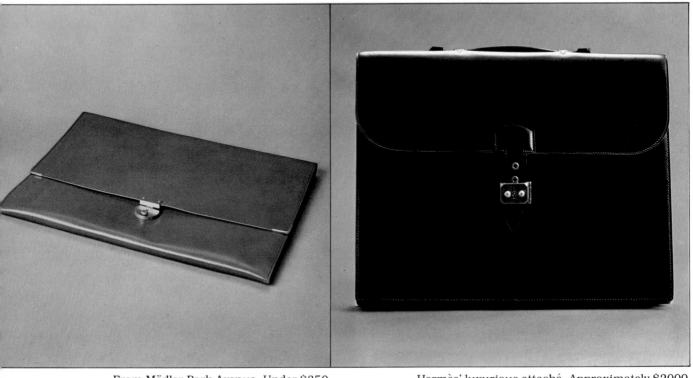

From Mädler Park Avenue. Under $350.

Hermès' luxurious attaché. Approximately $2000.

Beautiful accessories that can organize your life.

From Mark Cross, a memo pad.
Over $100.

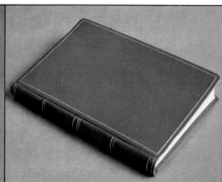

A manuscript book from
T. Anthony. Under $100.

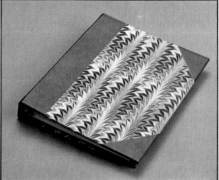

This address book from ffolio 72
can be covered in your favorite
paper or fabric. Under $35.

Here the ffolio 72 address book is
covered in gray snakeskin.
Approximately $50.

A wallet diary from *The Economist*
even includes a section of useful
information. Approximately $25.

The Economist desk diary includes
international information.
Approximately $45.

From Bottega Veneta, an agenda.
Under $250.

The Bottega Veneta agenda, open.

S. T. Dupont jotter in tan leather
with china-ink black border.
Approximately $75.

Bottega Veneta's memo and address book. Under $100.

Styled precisely like the manila envelope, only in leather, from T. Anthony. Approximately $50.

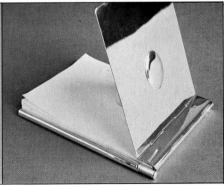

Bulgari's sterling silver notepad holder. Under $500.

A desk-sized weekly agenda from Bottega Veneta. Under $200.

This notebook of grained calf, from Lancel. Approximately $80.

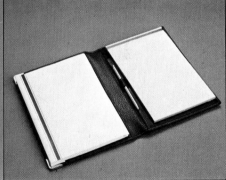

Gucci's phone desk planner. Approximately $125.

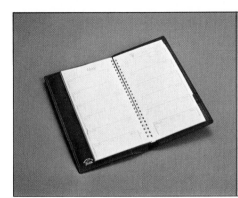

Gucci's pocket diary, covered in pigskin. Under $100.

A brightly colored desk organizer from Leathersmith, Ltd. Approximately $125.

Better than In-Out boxes, these custom-covered folders from ffolio 72. Approximately $25 each.

Timepieces are for information, not decoration. Big clocks are clunky. A clock should be small and inconspicuous, though not so small it can't be read.

Tiffany & Co. Under $200.

Top, Concord electric desk clock. Under $300.
Center, Gübelin gilt and lacquer finish. Under $150.
Bottom, Tiffany & Co. gold alarm clock. Under $200.

Top, Concord 2⅜-inch clock. Approximately $250.
Center, Tortoise-shell clock by Hermès. Approximately $600.
Bottom, Tiffany & Co. gilt with red numbers. Approximately $150.

Top, Gübelin, octagonal eight-day clock. Under $150.
Center, Van Cleef & Arpels chrome and gold plated alarm clock. $650.
Bottom, Cartier burgundy clock. Approximately $250.

Two superb examples of cabinetry enclosing timepieces. The Patek Philippe small Naviquartz gilt marine chronometer is from Tiffany and is encased in mahogany with accents of brass. Approximately $3500.

Tiffany & Co.'s Baume & Mercier carriage clock. The octagonal case is of pearwood with brass fittings and a brass inscription plate. The clock comes with a pigskin carrying case. Approximately $3000.

Pen and pencil sets are for graduations and retirements. Keep your extra pens and pencils in a drawer or in an attractive pencil cup. If you've got a good-looking fountain pen or an elegant ballpoint, flaunt it. The pens and pencils shown here range in price from the seventy-nine-cent Flair pen—an example of good design when price is no object—to the over-$2000 eighteen-karat-gold "ruler pen" from Bulgari.

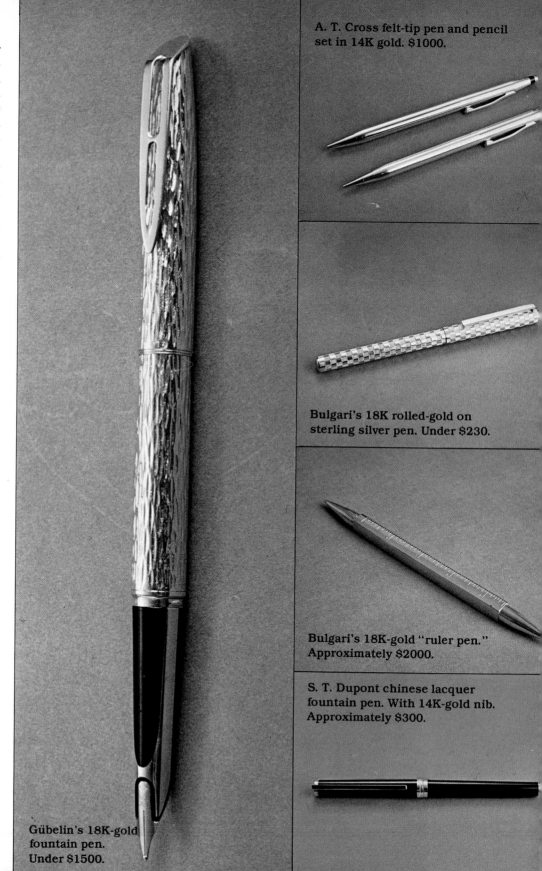

A. T. Cross felt-tip pen and pencil set in 14K gold. $1000.

Bulgari's 18K rolled-gold on sterling silver pen. Under $230.

Bulgari's 18K-gold "ruler pen." Approximately $2000.

S. T. Dupont chinese lacquer fountain pen. With 14K-gold nib. Approximately $300.

Gübelin's 18K-gold fountain pen. Under $1500.

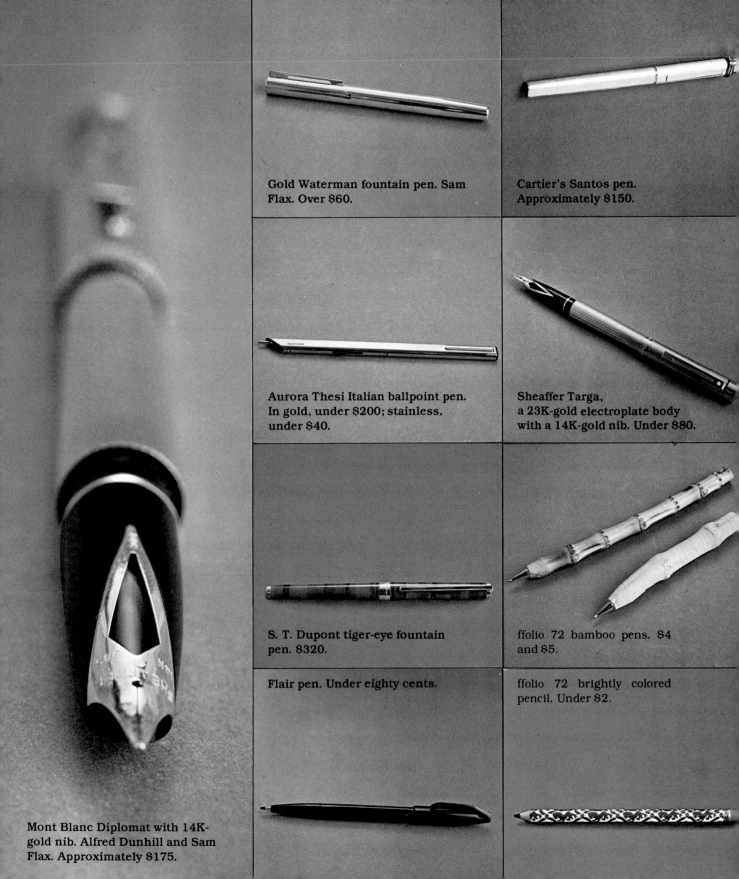

Gold Waterman fountain pen. Sam Flax. Over $60.

Cartier's Santos pen. Approximately $150.

Aurora Thesi Italian ballpoint pen. In gold, under $200; stainless, under $40.

Sheaffer Targa, a 23K-gold electroplate body with a 14K-gold nib. Under $80.

S. T. Dupont tiger-eye fountain pen. $320.

ffolio 72 bamboo pens. $4 and $5.

Flair pen. Under eighty cents.

ffolio 72 brightly colored pencil. Under $2.

Mont Blanc Diplomat with 14K-gold nib. Alfred Dunhill and Sam Flax. Approximately $175.

As a general rule, the only electronic equipment on a desk should be the telephone. These dictating machines, though, are slim and trim enough to fit into an attaché case or even a flat portfolio.

Left page: Close-up of the Sony BM-12, 15 ounces.

with electronic indexing. The pocket-sized recorder can record continuously for up to eight hours and also can record directly from a radio or television. Under $370.

Above left is the side view of the Sony BM-12.

At right is the smallest

Sony ever—the Sony BM-500, weighing in at 9 ounces. The rugged little recorder is protected by an attractive black all-metal case, making it perfect for dictating while you're jogging or playing tennis. Under $300.

Above left is the pocket-size Micromite from Dictaphone, featuring a "Q-Alert" system that lets your secretary know, when transcribing, how long each letter is. Under $300.

Above right, you can't get any lighter than this. Norelco's 640 Impromptu pocket recorder weighs 6.5 ounces. Approximately $325.

On the facing page, top, the Norelco UltraSlim Executive Notetaker weighs 8.2 ounces and is only three-quarters of an inch thick. Optional accessories include a telephone adaptor and a conference micro-

phone. Approximately $275.
Bottom, IBM's Executive
Recorder is competitively
priced under $200.

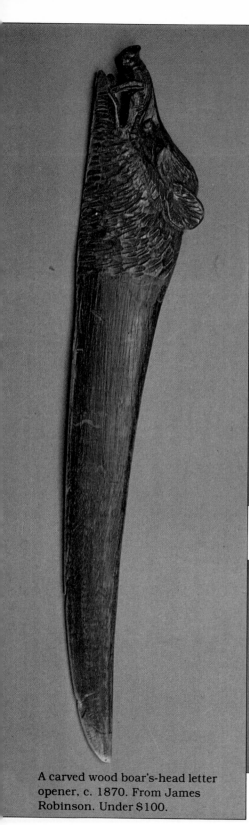

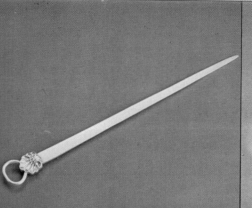

A George III silver shell skewer, now a letter opener. James Robinson. Under $750.

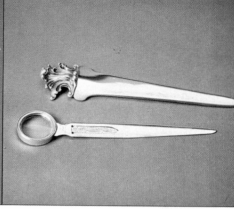

Buccellati: A handmade silver letter opener; a magnifying glass/bookmark/ letter opener. Price unavailable.

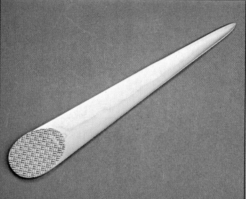

Gübelin's 18K yellow gold and stainless steel letter opener. Approximately $450.

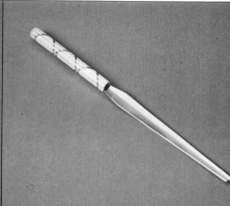

Cartier's sterling silver letter opener with fluted handle and 18K-gold ribbon work. Approximately $300.

A carved wood boar's-head letter opener, c. 1870. From James Robinson. Under $100.

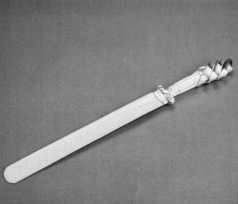

A Victorian silver-mounted ivory paper knife, c. 1889. James Robinson. Approximately $375.

A Victorian carved and painted wood seal from James II Galleries at James Robinson. Under $150.

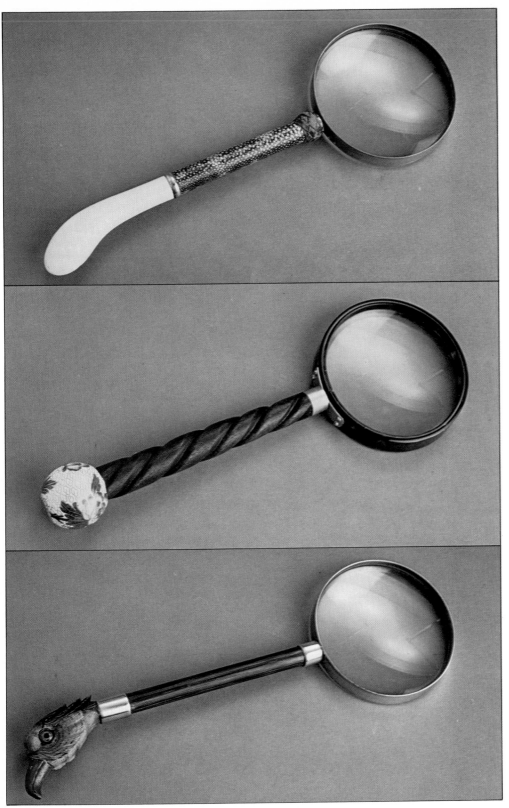

The perfect desk ornaments are as functional as they are decorative.

Featured on this page are Victorian magnifying glasses, all from the James II Galleries at James Robinson, approximately $300 each. At top, a shagreen and ivory handle. Middle, tortoise and porcelain handle. And bottom, carved wooden handle.

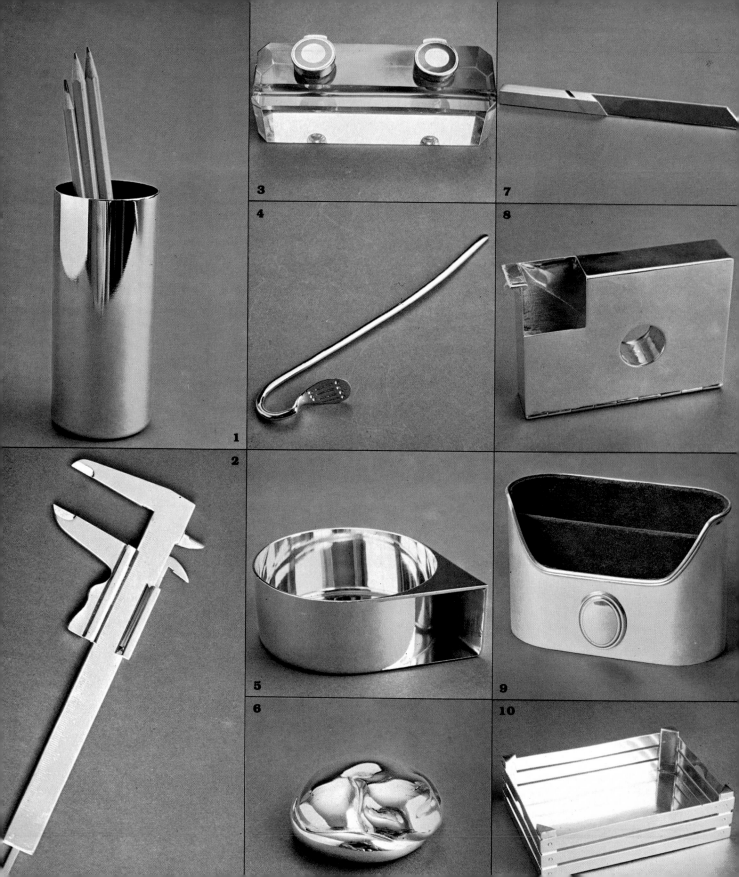

On both pages, a potpourri of beautiful yet functional desk accessories.

1 Polished-chrome pencil holder—TSAO Designs.

2 Sterling silver architectural ruler—Mark Cross.

3 An Edwardian silver and enamel mounted glass inkwell—James II Galleries.

4 Gold-plated bookmark—Mark Cross.

5 A sterling silver bowl which can be used as an ashtray or paper clip holder—Bulgari.

6 Sterling silver sleeping cat paperweight—Tiffany.

7 Sterling silver and 18K gold inlaid letter opener—Bulgari.

8 Sterling silver Scotch tape holder—Tiffany.

9 Sterling silver letter holder lined in midnight-blue velvet—Cartier.

10 Small silver openwork basket to hold business cards—Tiffany.

At right, three ashtrays from TSAO Designs.

11 Polished greenstone marble.

12 Polished chrome.

13 Polished black marble.

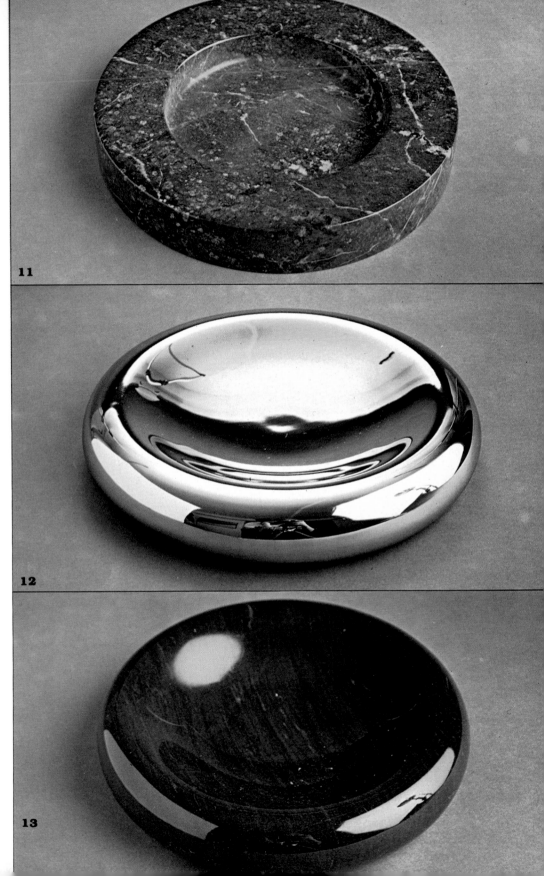

Directory

Prices are as accurate as possible at the time of publication. The objects are subject to prior sale and all prices are approximate. Addresses are listed at the end of Directory.

Desks

Page 12

Robert Fomon, Chairman and
Chief Executive Officer
E. F. Hutton & Company Inc.
New York, New York

Desk Antique Regency
Wing chair Antique Chippendale
Conference table Contemporary
rosewood and lacquer, B&B
America
Conference chairs Brno chairs,
Knoll International
Lounge chairs B&B America
Coffee table Original design of
honed granite and Kortan steel, by
Ronald Bricke & Associates, Inc.
Oriental rug Antique Heriz;
Morjikian
Trees Ficus
Thermal veil shades Homecraft
Painting E. F. Hutton portrait; E.
F. Hutton collection
Floor Pirelli rubber tile
Walls Loden cloth; Austria
Desk blotter Christie's—London
Designed by Ronald Bricke &
Associates, Inc.
333 East 69th Street
New York, New York 10021
(212) 472-9006

Page 14

Erwin Isman, President
Perry Ellis Sportswear, Inc.
New York, New York

Desk Hand-lacquered English
sycamore, custom designed by
James Terrell
Desk chair Eames chair/Herman
Miller
Pull-up chairs Mies van der Rohe
Carpet Harmony
Credenza English sycamore,
custom designed by James Terrell,
built by Anton Waldman &
Associates

Page 15

Secretary's office
Desk Custom designed by James
Terrell
Chair Eames chair/Herman Miller
Light Luxo
Carpet Harmony
Designed by James E. Terrell AIA
Hambrecht Terrell Interiors
Corporation
419 East 50th Street
New York, New York 10022
(212) 888-1758

Page 16

Ralph Destino, President
Cartier, Inc.
New York, New York

Desk Louis XV–style
Desk chairs Auffray & Co.
Curtains Stroheim & Romann
Wall covering Wolf-Gordon
suedecloth
Bronze mirror New Deal Glass
Side shelving unit Cado Royal
System
Sofa and club chair Stroheim &
Romann fabric, off-white wool;
upholstered by Cavaleri Bros.
Designed by Ray Mastrobuoni
In-House Interior Designer
Cartier, New York

Page 18

Walter Hoving, Chairman
Tiffany & Co.
New York, New York

Desk Leather-topped 18th-century
mahogany partner's desk
Chairs Chippendale
Bowls on desk Lowestoft
Box on desk Vermeil
Engagement book cover Vermeil
Fabric for curtains and upholstery
Printed Belgian linen, by
Eaglesham Prints
Overhead light Stainless steel with
glass lens

Page 20

Estée Lauder, Chairman
Estée Lauder, Inc.
New York, New York

Desk Louis XVI
Wing chairs Louis XVI, antique
slate-blue silk velvet fabric from Old
World Weavers
Red chairs French, Second Empire
Couch Belle Epoch style, in oyster-
colored silk taffeta, from Clarence
House
Lamp desk 18th-century French
Bouillotte
Large mirror Venetian, early 19th
century
Console table Louis XVI
Vases Ancient Chinese
Wall covering Soft blue hand-
painted Oriental rice paper from
Gracie & Co.
Mementoes Front, Crystal Apple,
Association for a Better New York,
1977; right, 1974 and 1977

Fragrance Foundation Hall of Fame
Awards; center, 1975 Annual
Fashion Award, Pogue's; left top,
1977 Legendary Woman Award,
Birmingham-Southern College; left
bottom, sculpture by Charles Gene
Moore

Page 24

Ira Howard Levy, Senior Vice
President of Corporate Marketing-
Design
Estée Lauder, Inc.
New York, New York

Desk Mr. Levy's design;
cantilevered mahogany and birch
inlay.
Desk chair Ergon high-back
Executive chair by Herman Miller.
Upholstered in seal-colored Hermes
Leather. Polished-aluminum base.
Chairs Signed Sheraton, 18th
century
Translucent window shades
Elizabeth Scott fabric
Square-shade floor lamp
Castalleone, Milan
Floors Diagonal lime-pickled oak
Wall covering Hand-loomed Irish
wool, Dublin
**Contemporary impressionist
painting** Robert Dash
Screwdriver sculpture David
Hamberger Inc.
Organizer box Swiss folk art, late
17th century
Floral arrangement Fellan Florist
Ashtray Georgian warmer plate
Mugs Devin Countryhouse
Address book "Great Addresses,"
designed by Ira Howard Levy,
published by The Museum of
Modern Art

Page 26

H. Ridgely Bullock, Chairman and
President
UMC Industries, Inc.
Stamford, Connecticut

Writing desk Kittinger Furniture
Company. With "burnt orange"
tooled Lackawanna leather top
Desk chair Kittinger
Armchairs Wood & Hogan. Covered
in Lackawanna leather, "burnt
orange"
Love seat Kittinger
Side chairs Kittinger
Antique architect's table Hyde
Park Antiques, N.Y.C.
Sofa Kittinger
Side table Wood & Hogan
Coffee table Chinese, in black
lacquer, from Paul Jones
Fabrics Brunschwig & Fils, N.Y.C.
Chest Pie crust table, Wood &
Hogan
Fabric on walls, draperies
Scalamandré

Upholstered furniture Joseph
Giannola, N.Y.C.
All furniture in English 18th-
century style
Designed by Carlyle Lind, Inc.
446 East 52nd Street
New York, New York 10022
(212) 688-8272

Page 27

John T. Rettaliata, Chairman
Banco di Roma
Chicago, Illinois

Square desk Custom designed;
mfg. by Woodwork Corp. African
rosewood, trimmed in mirror-
polished stainless steel
Paintings T. Oti Scialoja (3 oils)
Guest chairs Zographos
Leather telephone console Italian
leather with recessed telephone
and retractable cord
Designed by Robert D.
Kleinschmidt, when at Skidmore,
Owings & Merrill/Chicago
Now with: Powell/Kleinschmidt,
Inc.
115 South La Salle Street
Chicago, Illinois 60603
(312) 726-2208

Page 27

Arch Nadler, Chairman
Nadler & Larimer, Inc.
New York, New York

Desk Pace
Desk chair Turner
Credenza Pace
Glass table Apollo (custom)
Sofa and matching chairs Stendig
Painting behind sofa Ira Schwartz
Pull-up chairs Turner
Designed by Wilke Davis Associates
522 Fifth Avenue
New York, New York 10036
(212) 840-7090

Page 28

Edward E. Elson, President
Elson's and Atlanta News
Agency, Inc.
Atlanta, Georgia

Club chairs Le Corbusier. Atelier
International
Lounge chair Le Corbusier.
Covered in pony skin. Atelier
International
Walls Stainless-steel paneled
Floors Teak parquet
Rug 18th-century Chinese
Marble cube table-desk Designed
by architect
Telephone table Art deco octagonal
table, in the style of Dufrene
Steel cabinets Edgar Brandt
Painting Whitney Leland.
Items on the coffee table
K. Hagenauer brass mirror
Silver Cartier pen
Tiffany & Co. silver box

Buccellati letter opener
Leather writing case, Mark Cross
Vase, Nancy Daum
In the cabinets Brass and steel figures by K. Hagenauer
Bookends by Chase
Vase by Longwy
Flask by Muller Frères
Lalique decanter
Clock by Le Coultre
Vases by Primavera
Designed by Irv Weiner, Architect
1800 Peachtree Center South
Atlanta, Georgia 30303
(404) 522-8811

Page 30

Didier Aaron, Inc.
Parquetry desk Italian 18th century (Louis XV); tulip wood, violet veneered, with ormolu mounts. Formerly in the Russian Imperial Collection.
H: 30½″ W: 69″ D: 34½″
Price: Approximately $95,000

Page 32

Ward Bennett Designs for Brickel Associates Inc.
"I-Beam" table with overhang
Black-enameled steel pedestal base, cremo or white Italian marble; wood tops and plastic tops available on request.
Item #3093
Top: W: 30″ D: 30″ H: 16″
Base: W: 16″ D: 16″ H: 15¼″
Price: Approximately $1500

Page 34

Stair & Company Inc.
Chippendale writing table
Mahogany with brass fret brackets, c. 1760
Item #A7354
W: 50″ D: 30″ H: 30″
Price: Approximately $26,000

Page 35

Dunbar
dePolo/Dunbar desk
Shown with granite top and leather body, the desk is also available with pedestals, or with return. Options available on this piece are marble instead of granite, desk made entirely in English oak (natural, medium, dark), or leather top with lacquer or leather body.
Item #7840
W: 69″ D: 33″ H: 28½″
Price: $2500 to $9000

Page 36

Didier Aaron, Inc.
Desk of the "Collectionneur"
Rosewood veneer with ivory handles and sabots. The prototype of this desk was made for the Hôtel du Collectionneur at the Arts

Décoratifs Exhibition of 1925.
Signed J. E. Ruhlmann
W: 55½″ D: 30″
Price: Approximately $50,000

Page 38

Kittinger Furniture Company
George Washington desk
Exact reproduction, mahogany, light heirloom finish
Item #416-1-2
W: 72″ D: 36″
Price: Approximately $5500

Page 40

Atelier International, Ltd.
Marcatré Executive
Natural ash wood pedestal-base table with black leather inserts. Desks available with or without leather writing inserts.
Item #2020101
H: 29″ W: 40″ L: 79″
Designed by Giovanni Carini
Price: Approximately $4000

Page 41

Top
Jordan-Volpe Gallery
Trestle table
Made of fumed quarter-sawn white oak, c. 1910. Designed and executed by Leopold and J. George Stickley, Fayetteville, New York
H: 29″ D: 44″ L: 72″
Price: Approximately $8500

Bottom
Jordan-Volpe Gallery
Library table
Mahogany desk with hand-hammered copper pulls; signed with paper label c. 1905–6
Executed by Gustav Stickley's craftsman workshops, Eastwood, New York
H: 29″ W: 24″ D: 31½″
Price: Approximately $10,000

Page 42

Hyde Park Antiques, Ltd.
Adams writing table
A rare writing table, double-sided, with an additional pull-out writing surface. A golden hue of faded and patined mahogany.
W: 54″ D: 32″ H: 32″
Price: Approximately $18,000

Page 43

Atelier International, Ltd.
LC 6 table
Designed by Le Corbusier; available with glass or wood top, base of welded oval tubing.
W: 90″ D: 33½″ H: 27⅛″
Price: Approximately $2000

Page 44

Smith & Watson Inc.
Hepplewhite style writing table
Antique brown mahogany
Item #F-4
W: 54″ D: 28½″ H: 30″
Price: Approximately $3100

Page 45

Wood & Hogan Inc.
Chippendale style writing table made in England
Mahogany with hand-tooled leather top
Item #B1329
W: 60″ D: 31″ H: 30″
Price: Approximately $5500

Page 46

Vladimir Kagan Designs, Inc.
Olympic desk
Garnet high-polish lacquer
Item #7801
W: 72″ D: 36″ H: 29″
Price: Approximately $15,000

Page 48

Ward Bennett Designs for Brickel Associates Inc.
Desk-conference table
Leather-covered
Item #3803
H: 28¾″ W: 78″ D: 36″
Price: Approximately $2500

Page 50

Didier Aaron, Inc.
Folding desk
Mahogany traveling desk bearing the coat of arms of Czar Paul I of Russia. Made by David Roentgen (Master in 1780)
H: 39½″ W: 33″ D: 18″
Price: Approximately $150,000

Chairs

Page 54

**David Rockefeller, Chairman
Chase Manhattan Bank, N.A.
New York, New York**

Conference table Designed by Ward Bennett for Lehigh-Leopold; custom wood, steel base
Swivel chairs Designed by Ward Bennett for Lehigh-Leopold; upholstery in tan leather, American Leather Co.
Rug Tai ping
Upholstered furniture Granick, in Jack Lenor Larsen neutral textured fabrics
Desk English elm burl, designed by Skidmore, Owings & Merrill. Made by John Scalia Schmieg & Kotzian
Floors Teak
Selected paintings Juan Gris,

Fruit Dish, Glass and Newspaper, oil on wood, 1916; Juan Gris, *Green Cloth*, oil on canvas, 1925; Henri Matisse, *Still Life with Grapes*, oil on canvas, c. 1898; Kenzo Okada, *Homage*, oil on canvas, 1960; Andrew Wyeth, *River Cove*, tempera on masonite, no date; Mark Rothko, *White Center*
Selected art objects
Japanese: priest's robe, brocade, no date; Jizo figure, carved wood, early Kamakura, 12th century; traveling shrine, late 17th, early 18th century, Buddha and hierarchy.
Chinese: ceramic bowl, yellow glaze, Ming, Wan Li period, 1580–1620; plate, 14th century, design from 11th century, Ch'u-chou, celadon glaze.
Korean: bowl, 12–13th century, ceramic, dark olive green glaze, Koryu dynasty; Buddha, c. 1200, Koryu dynasty, Songdo, bronze.
Indian: temple dancer, Hindu, South India, late 19th century, bronze.
Indo-Persian: Mosul incense burner, 18th century, bronze.
Greek: amphora, black-figured, Attic, c. 540 B.C.; lekythos, red-figured, Apulian, 4th century B.C.; two toy hydriae, red-figured, Apulian, 4th century B.C.; amphora, red-figured, Attic, 370–350 B.C.; lekythos, red-figured, Attic, 470 B.C.; lekythos, black-figured, Paestum, 5th century B.C.; lekythos, black-figured, Attic, c. 470 B.C.
Roman: bottle, 1st–2nd century, glass.
African: antelope, Western Sudan, Bambara tribe, wood, no date.
Melanesian: paddle, Northeast New Guinea, upper Sepik River, May River, wood, no date.
German: contemporary sculpture by Willi Gutman
Designed by Skidmore, Owings & Merrill
400 Park Avenue
New York, New York 10022
(212) 759-2121
Special Consultant Ward Bennett, consultant on furniture and furnishings.

Page 58

**Diane Von Furstenberg, Chairman
Diane Von Furstenberg, Inc.
New York, New York**

Desk Art nouveau
Armchairs Art deco
Carpet Carpet Showrooms
Fabrics Scalamandré
Shades Maharem
Drapery Contour Drapery
Designed by Diane Von Furstenberg with Edward J. Robusto, formerly of The Switzer Group, Inc., now

Edward J. Robusto, Designer
310 Greenwich Street
New York, New York 10013
(212) 732-5555

Page 60

David T. Kearns, President
Xerox Corporation
Stamford, Connecticut

Desk Eckert & Johnson, custom
Executive chair Metropolitan
Pull-up chairs Helikon, fabric by Scalamandré
Credenza Eckert & Johnson, custom
Carpet Patrick Mills, custom color
Sofa Stendig
Lounge chairs Stendig, fabric by Isabel Scott
Coffee table Apollo
Painting behind sofa John Gundelfinger, *Sunset After Thundershowers—Delaware River Valley*, 1979; oil on canvas, 50″ x 72″
Designed by ISD, Inc.
866 Third Avenue
New York, New York
(212) 751-0800

Page 62

John Marion, President
Sotheby Parke Bernet Inc.
New York, New York

Desk Late George III mahogany pedestal desk
Paintings, clockwise from top left Pierre Bonnard, *Woman in a Bathtub*, c. 1917; Pierre-Auguste Renoir, *The Loge*, 1897; Renoir, *Bather Drying Her Feet*, c. 1907
Sculpture Bronze bust of Lincoln by Max Bachman, copyright 1909 (Gorham Co. Founders)
Chairs Regency mahogany armchairs, early 19th century

page 64

Ahmet Ertegun, Chairman
Atlantic Recording Corporation
New York, New York

Desk Karl Springer
Chair Knoll International/Pollock
Pull-up chairs Knoll International/Pollock
Wall units John Beringer
Carpenter Langenbacher
Sofa Ray Murray
Print Rauschenberg
Designed by Mica Ertegun and Chessy Rayner of Mac II
125 East 81 Street
New York, New York 10028
(212) 249-4466

Page 66

Geraldine Stutz, President
Henri Bendel
New York, New York

Desk Origin unknown; it has been in the office for the past 20 years
Rattan chairs Deutsch
Objects on desk Presents, mementos, and awards of personal meaning to Ms. Stutz.
Round storage basket Banana
Fabric for round table Clarence House
Fabric for banquette, pillows and chairs Vice Versa. Studio M did the upholstery
Coffee table Designed by Mario Buatta. Custom made by Karl Springer
Wall lamps Lightolier
Alfred Jensen lithographs Pace Gallery
Armoire Designed by H. McKim Glazebrook
Plants Renny Reynolds
Gauze curtains Fabric from Vice Versa
Painted bamboo blinds Bamboo & Rattan Works in Hoboken, N.J.
Fashion illustrations and bound volumes Found in a closet in the store, they had belonged to Mr. Henri Bendel, who was a collector of fashion books and magazines.
Painting on wood of Henri Bendel Joel Schumacher
Water pitcher Hammacher Schlemmer
Shell-shaped ashtrays B. Altman
Designed by Mario Buatta, Geraldine Stutz and Robert Rufino

Page 68

Lee H. Berendt, President
Commodity Exchange, Inc.
New York, New York

Oval table-desk Cumberland Furniture Corporation
Desk chair Atelier International, Ltd., The Tecno Collection
Guest chairs Krueger
Special built-in wall unit John Langenbacher Co., Inc.
Designed by Bonsignore Brignati & Mazzotta, P.C. Architects
370 Seventh Avenue
New York, New York 10001
(212) 868-9200

Page 70

Larry Nachman, President
Swirl Inc.
New York, New York

Table Don Rousseau, New York
Fan Hunter Ventilating Fans
Sculpture Raphael Martini
Pull-up chairs Knoll
Desk chair Antique English, mahogany and leather, c. 1840; from Royal Antiques, New Orleans
Painting behind desk By William Aiken Walker; from Schindler's Antiques, Charleston, South Carolina
Designed by Gwathmey Siegel &

Associates, Architects
154 West 57th Street
New York, New York 10019
(212) 489-9280

Page 72

Dunbar
dePolo/Dunbar chair
Gray glove leather
Item #7860
H: 32″ W: 27½″ D: 27½″
Price: $1600, plus fabric

Page 73

Karl Springer
Swivel chair
Upholstered in any fabric, memory swivel, metal base
Designed by Karl Springer
24½″ diameter base
Price: $2300, plus fabric

Page 74

Atelier International, Ltd.
LC2 chair
Highly polished tubing and angle steel is hand-formed and bent. Chair cushions are varying densities of polyurethane and Dacron. Available in a full selection of AI fabric, vinyls, or leathers, leather piping
Designed by Le Corbusier
H: 26.4″ W: 29.9″ D: 27.5″
Price: $1775 to $2660, plus fabric

Page 75

Top left
Knoll International
Armchair
Steel-rod frame with nickel finish, available in various coverings
Item #1725
W: 26½″ D: 22″ H: 29″
Price: Approximately $1000, plus fabric

Bottom left
Knoll International
Brno chair
Flat stainless steel, polished finish, upholstery over hardwood frame with foam seat on spring suspension
Item #255
Designed by Mies van der Rohe
W: 23″ D: 23″ H: 31″
Price: Approximately $1100 to $1400, plus fabric

Top right
Knoll International
Armchair
Frame and arms: thin laminations of wood veneer, available in a variety of finishes. Shell: molded plastic. Upholstery: inside and outside can be covered in same material
Item #1305
Designed by William Stephens

W: 22⅛″ D: 22½″ H: 32″
Price: Approximately $500, plus fabric

Bottom right
Knoll International
Swivel armchair
Base: cast aluminum, adjustable swivel and tilt mechanism. Frame: cast aluminum. Upholstery: foam cushions
Item #2348
Designed by Andrew Ivar Morrison and Bruce R. Hannah
W: 24″ D: 25¾″ H: 36″/38¾″
Price: $500 to $800, plus fabric

Page 76

Ward Bennett Designs for Brickel Associates Inc.
Low-arm side chair
Round carved wood frame, oiled natural ash; open sides, French-style upholstery, tight seat
Item #1132
W: 23″ D: 23½″ H: 32½″
Price: Approximately $1100, plus fabric

Page 77

Ward Bennett Designs for Brickel Associates Inc.
Round carved wood frame armchair, caned
Oiled natural ash frame, natural caned seat and back, loose knife-edge seat cushion
Item #1078
W: 25″ D: 23½″ H: 30¾″
Price: Approximately $1100, plus fabric

Page 78

Left
Ward Bennett Designs for Brickel Associates Inc.
Mobius Executive Armchair
Oiled natural ash, low-back carved wood frame, mirror-plated steel pedestal, tilt swivel with profile casters; fully upholstered, semi-attached knife-edge seat cushion on caned wood
Item #1150
W: 25″ D: 23¾″ H: 32¾″
Price: Approximately $1600, plus fabric

Right
Ward Bennett Designs for Brickel Associates Inc.
Upholstered armchair
Pedestal tilt-swivel with profile casters. Loose knife-edge seat cushion, mirror-plated steel base
Item #1101
W: 26″ D: 26½″ H: 33″
Price: Approximately $1100

Page 79

Knoll International
Small swivel armchair
Base: stainless steel cap over steel armature, adjustable swivel and tilt

mechanism. Upholstery: foam rubber over molded plastic shells
Designed by Max Pearson
Item #1808
W: 25½″ D: 25″ H: 33″/36″
Price: Approximately $800 plus fabric

Page 80

Atelier International, Ltd.
Barbar Management chairs
Tilt-swivel, adjustable height, gas-filled pressure cylinder, casters, five-foot base, with arms
Item #2651-40
Designed by Andre Vandenbeuck
Price: $750, plus fabric

Page 81

Jack Lenor Larsen
Ritz armchair
Solid maple frame, hardwood seat panel, flame retardant foam in seat and back·
Item #6000
Designed by Ben Baldwin
W: 20½″ D: 17½″ H: 33⅜″
Price: Approximately $660

Page 82

Zographos Designs Limited
Lounge chair
Fully upholstered in fabric or leather
Item #CH92
W: 30″ D: 31″ H: 32″
Price: $1300, plus fabric

Page 83

Zographos Designs Limited
Bucket chair
Leather cover, polished stainless steel or bronze base
Item #CH72
W: 24″ D: 25″ H: 32″
Price: $1650, plus fabric

Page 84

Ward Bennett Designs for Brickel Associates Inc.
U-Chair
All upholstered; tight poly/Dacron seat
Item #2004
W: 31″ D: 28¾″ H: 23¼″
Price: $1300, plus fabric

Page 85

Ward Bennett Designs for Brickel Associates Inc.
U-Chair
All upholstered; loose poly/Dacron seat cushion; profile casters
Item #2001
W: 31″ D: 28¾″ H: 23¼″
Price: $1500, plus fabric

Page 86

Top
Ward Bennett Designs for Brickel Associates Inc.
U-Settee
All upholstered; tight poly/Dacron seat
Item #2006
W: 60″ D: 28¾″ H: 23¼″
Price: Approximately $1850, plus fabric

Bottom left
Ward Bennett Designs for Brickel Associates Inc.
Cartouche sofa
All upholstered low seating
Item #2532
D: 32¼″ H: 25″ W: 85″
Price: Approximately $3450, plus fabric

Page 88

Bernard & S. Dean Levy Inc.
Queen Anne corner chair
Made of cherry wood, Rhode Island origin, c. 1740–50
Price: Approximately $28,500

Page 89

Florian Papp Inc.
George III Sheraton mahogany exercise chair
English, c. 1790–1800
Price: Approximately $4800

Page 90

Top left
Knoll International
Swivel armchair
Base: stainless steel cap over steel armature, adjustable swivel and tilt mechanism. Upholstery, arms: solid black plastic
Item #1258
Designed by Charles Pollock
W: 26¼″ D: 27″ H: 30¼″/33¼″
Price: $565 to $700, plus fabric

Top right
Thonet
Brno chair
Item #4838
Polished chrome-plated tubular steel
Designed by Mies van der Rohe
W: 22″ D: 24″ H: 29½″
Price: $270, plus fabric

Bottom right
Florian Papp Inc.
Windsor armchair
Yew wood, spindle back; Flemish, early 19th century
Price: Approximately $3000

Page 91

The Incurable Collector, a subsidiary of Stair & Company Inc.
Chinese chair

One of a set of six Chinese lacquer chairs, c. 1810
Item: A6890
Price: $23,000 for the six

Tables

Page 94

**Paul C. Harper, Jr., Chairman
Needham Harper & Steers
Advertising, Inc.
New York, New York**

Dining Room
Table Zographos
Chairs Zographos
Settee Knoll International
Upholstery Schumacher
Drum coffee tables Apollo
Photos By Ansel Adams: left, *Pinnacles*, the Alabama Hills in Owens Valley, California, 1945; middle, *Fog*, Cascade Pass in Washington, 1945; right, *Mount Williamson*, Sierra Nevada, Manganar, California, 1944
Painting Acrylic on canvas, untitled, by Byoung-O Min
Carpeting H. Lawrence Mills

Page 95

Office
Table-desk ISD custom designed
Wall-hung credenza ISD custom designed
Leather-wrapped storage cube ISD custom designed
Corner cube-table ISD custom designed
Visitors' chairs Knoll International/Brno
Sofa Stendig
Club chairs Stendig
Darius coffee table Stendig
Upholstery American Leather
Carpet beige wool cut-pile H. Lawrence Mills
Tapestry Grassinos
Small bronze sculpture Bertoia

Designed by ISD
866 Third Avenue
New York, New York 10022
(212) 751-0800

Page 96

**Katharine Graham,
Chairman of the Board
The Washington Post Company
Washington, D.C.**

Office
Guest chairs ICF, upholstered in taupe suede
Sofa Knoll International, in off-white wool upholstery
Lounge chairs Knoll International, in off-white wool upholstery
Carpet Tai Ping, off-white wool
Drapery Isabel Scott; off-white Verel
Woodcut Carol Summers, *Hellesport*

Page 97

Dining Room
Dining table Lehigh-Leopold custom; opaque lacquer top
Dining chairs Knoll International/Don Petitt
Carpet Thaibok silk
China "Blue Danube"
Designed by Ford and Earl Design Associates
28820 Mound Road
Warren, Michigan 48090
(313) 539-2280

Page 98

**Eugene J. Grossman, Principal
Anspach Grossman Portugal
New York, New York**

Files Supreme
Executive chair Knoll International/Pollock
Guest chairs Knoll International
Conference table Apollo; leather top with restaurant base
Lamps Luxo
Mini blinds Levelor
Designed by Bray-Schaible Design Inc.
80 West 40th Street
New York, New York 10018
(212) 354-7525

Page 100

**Conference Room
Interconnect Planning
Corporation
New York, New York**

Conference table Designed by Rubin and Smith-Miller; Russo Verde marble
Chairs Brno, Knoll International
Carpet Goodlin Industries
Floor Quarry tile, American Olean Tile Co.
Designed by Michael Rubin and Henry Smith-Miller
305 Canal Street
New York, New York 10013
(212) 966-5963

Page 102

**Boardroom
General American Life Insurance Company
St. Louis, Missouri**

Triangular table Designed by Philip Johnson; top 3-inch-thick pink granite from Italy, brass base
Chairs JG
Walls Brown Ultrasuede
Paintings Louis Stein, acrylic on canvas
Designed by Johnson-Burgee Architects
375 Park Avenue
New York, New York 10022
(212) 751-7440

Page 104

Boardroom
Banco di Roma
Chicago, Illinois

Table Designed by Robert D.
Kleinschmidt; top, red Levanto
marble from Italy, steel base
Chairs Zographos
Carpet Custom-loomed. Based on
diamond shaped column of
building
Painting T. Oti Scialoja
Designed by Robert D.
Kleinschmidt, while at Skidmore,
Owings & Merrill, Chicago
Now with: Powell/Kleinschmidt,
Inc.
115 South LaSalle Street
Chicago, Illinois 60603
(312) 726-2208

Page 106

Boardroom
First Atlanta Corporation
Atlanta, Georgia

Table Walnut, 6′ x 36″ custom built
by John Scalia Schmieg & Kotzian
Chairs Custom designed by John
Scalia Schmieg & Kotzian
Chandelier From the old
boardroom, originally 1929
Carpet Antique Tabriz palace
carpet from Coury Rugs, Inc., N.Y.
Paintings Portraits of former
presidents and chairmen of the
bank from 1865 to 1977
Paneling Pine woodwork from the
old boardroom, 1929
Designed by Robert Malderez for
Eleanore LeMaire Associates (now
LeMaire Associates)
745 Fifth Avenue
New York, New York 10022
Now with: Carter Howley Hale
Stores Inc.
550 South Flower Street
Los Angeles, California 90071
(213) 620-0150

Page 108

Dining Rooms
**J. Henry Schroder Bank & Trust
Company**
New York, New York

Gray Room
Table Burl wood; by Brueton
Chairs Pace
Place setting Royal Worcester bone
china with ultramarine, cobalt-blue
and gold-leaf band, and Schroder
family crest made specially for
Schroders (used throughout dining
rooms)
Wall unit Ferguson Sorrentino
Design Incorporated
Art Six Piccadilles, by Dieter Roth
(screenprints); Birthday Square,
by Joseph Albers (screenprint)

Page 109

Top
Green Room
Table Green marble/Verde Acceglio;
by Ferguson Sorrentino Design
Incorporated; base manufactured
by Apollo Woodworking, top by
Forno Marble
Chairs Knoll International/Mies
van der Rohe; custom-dyed leather
Wall unit Ferguson Sorrentino
Design Incorporated
Lithographs Marc Chagall

Page 110

Bottom
Red Room
Table Knoll International
Wall unit Ferguson Sorrentino
Design Incorporated
Chairs Knoll International
Art Untitled, 1971, by Larry Zox
(etching and aquatint); Flowers
Made of Paper and Black Ink, by
David Hockney (lithograph);
Coloured Flowers Made of Paper
and Ink, by David Hockney
(lithograph)
Designed by Ferguson Sorrentino
Design Incorporated
5 East 57th Street
New York, New York 10022
(212) 759-3965

Page 110

**Arthur Samuels, Jr., President
Golo Footwear Corporation
New York, New York**

Desk Custom made of Formica
laminate; designed by Barbara
Schwartz, A.S.I.D., and Barbara
Ross of Dexter Design
Chairs Knoll International/Pollock
Carpet Wonder Weave (of Creslan
Acrylic by American Cyanamid),
through Budd Looms, N.Y.C.
Plants Plant Associates, N.Y.C.
Wall covering Henry Calvin Fabrics
Photographs Arthur Samuels, Jr.
Designed by Dexter Design
133 East 58th Street
New York, New York 10022
(212) 752-2426

Page 112

**Boardroom and Executive
Reception Area
Crocker National Bank
Los Angeles, California**

Boardroom
Table Bartiki wood; Bert England
custom design, manufactured by
D & J Woodcraft
Chairs Umphreds
Ashtrays Dupont-Lohman
Casement draperies Ben Rose
Overdraperies Fortuny, Inc.
Carpet All-wool custom carpeting
by Salles

Page 113

Reception area
Desk Custom design by Bert
England
Chair J. Robert Scott
Upholstered furniture Martin/
Brattrud, Boris Kroll
Sofa Martin/Brattrud, fabric
by Art Com
Chairs Martin/Brattrud
Screen Chinese antique screen
Coffee table Baker Furniture
Designed by John Weeks, A.S.I.D.
Cannell & Chaffin Commercial
Interiors, Inc.
2843 West Seventh Street
Los Angeles, California 90005
(213) 380-7111

Page 114

**Executive Dining Room
E. F. Hutton & Company
New York, New York**

Table Gray granite, designed by
Gardner Lever
Chairs Stainless steel covered in
leather, by Gardner Lever
Carpet Ciseling rug, Stark Carpet;
braided rug, Patterson, Flynn &
Martin
Artwork Series of paper
constructions by Bilge
Friendlander
Wall unit Custom design by Ronald
Bricke & Associates
China Wedgewood
Silver Buccellati
Water globlets "Ultra" by Seneca
Glass
Wineglasses "Evora" by Black
Crystal

Page 115

Smaller Dining Room
Artwork Gray and yellow gouache
and crayon by Renaldo de Juan
Table Pink granite; by Gardner
Lever
Chairs Stainless steel and leather;
by Gardner Lever
Designed by Ronald Bricke &
Associates, Inc.
333 East 69th Street
New York, New York 10021
(212) 472-9006

Page 116

Sunar Ltd.
Race conference table
Top: imported Verde Antique
marble, 1½″ thick with bullnose
edge; choice of natural polished or
polyester finish
Base: 4″-D leg, 16-gauge steel with
³⁄₁₆″ stamped steel feet and dye-cast
zinc, chrome-plated caps
Finish: polyester painted finish,
black
Designed by Douglas Ball for Sunar

W: 40″ L: 80″ H: 29″
Price: Approximately $8100

Page 117

Thonet
Base: four-toe polished chrome
tubular base with self-leveling
glides
Top: self-edged plastic laminate top
Item #12M438
W: 42″ L: 42″ H: 30″
Price: $240

Page 118

Sunar Ltd.
Kyoto table
Beechwood with rosewood inlay,
adjustable legs snap into top
W: 45″ D: 45″ H: 14″
Price: Approximately $5000

Page 120

Karl Springer
Parchment dining table
Natural goatskin, parchment matte
finish
W: 46″ D: 48″ H: 29″
Price: Approximately $6000

Page 122

Knoll International
Table
Madera marble top with cast metal
pedestal, white fused finish
D: 48″ H: 28½″
Designed by Eero Saarinen
Item #176
Price: from $2200 to $3500

Page 123

Knoll International
Dining table
Base: solid wood or steel with
polished chrome
Top: wood veneer
Designed by Charles Pfister
Item #3014
Photographed here:
W: 47¼″ D: 47¼″ H: 28¾″
Size shown has been discontinued.
Table currently available in sizes:
W: 59″ D: 59″ H: 28¾″
(Approximately $4400–$5200)
W: 39⅜″ D: 39⅜″ H: 28¾″
(Approximately $2900–$3700)

Page 124

Castelli Furniture
LC table
Conference or executive table with
walnut top, chrome tubular base
W: 37¼″ L: 82½″ H: 28½″
(Available in other sizes)
Price: Approximately $1800

Page 126

Knoll International
Lunario table
½" tempered glass top; polished
steel base with counterbalance
weights
Designed by Cini Boeri
Item #52-201
W: 59" D: 44" H: 15¾"
Price: Approximately $2500

Page 128

Zographos Designs Limited
Conference table
Marble top, polished stainless steel
base
Item #TA 2-48M
D: 48" H: 29"
Price: Approximately $4700

Page 129

Zographos Designs Limited
Low coffee table
Polished glass, polished stainless
steel base
Item #TA42G
D: 42" H: 14"
Price: Approximately $1500

Page 130

Atelier International, Ltd.
Hardware/La Basilica
Natural Italian walnut or natural
ash wood
Designed by Mario Bellini
Price: Approximately $3800

Lighting

Page 134

George Barrie, Chairman,
President, and Chief Executive
Officer
Fabergé, Inc.
New York, New York

Source information
unavailable

Page 138

Masao Tsuyama, Chairman
California First Bank
San Francisco, California

Sofa Knoll, Pfister design
Chairs Knoll, Pfister design
Vertical blinds Levolar
Coffee table granite; by Zographos
Carpet Decorative Carpets, L.A.
Table next to sofa Ruby Carnelian
granite designed by Cedric
Hartman; in polished stainless
steel with bronze details
Designed by Charles Pfister for
Interior Design at
Skidmore, Owings & Merrill

1 Maritime Plaza
San Francisco, California 94111
(415) 981-1555

Page 140

J. Howard Johnson, President
Unitrex Division of Merchants
Corporation of America
New York, New York

Desk Custom design by Karl
Springer
Chair Vladimir Kagan
Sofa Henry Urban Inc.; fabric by
Clarence House
Coffee table Lacquered linen; RES
Manufacturing Corp.
Wing chair Antique, from Florian
Papp; fabric from Brunschwig &
Fils
Square upholstered chair Henry
Urban Inc.; fabric by Clarence
House
Carpet Dhurrie rug, from Rosecore
Carpets
Surrounds around windows Henry
Urban Inc.; fabric by Clarence
House
Designed by Robert Metzger
Interiors
275 Central Park West
New York, New York 10024
(212) 799-6740

Page 142

Dining Room
IBM Management Development
Center,
Armonk, New York

Tables Butcher's block tables by
John Adden
Chairs Claude Bunyard
Lighting Contemporary Ceilings
Carpet Harmony Carpet
Buffet and serving counter SKJS
Designed by Alan Goldberg/Eliot
Noyes, Associates
96 Main Street
New Canaan, Connecticut 06840
(203) 966-9561

Page 144

James T. Mills, Chairman
The Sperry and Hutchinson
Company
New York, New York

Carpet Barclay, by Bigelow–
Sanford
Sofa Covered in same fabric as
walls, from Gunlocke
Love seats Covered in same fabric
as walls, from Gunlocke
Coffee table Rectangular, Chinese
style; made of wood covered with
linen and lacquered in a vibrant
bittersweet; Roundtree Inc.
Wall hanging Designed by Leonard
Fisher. Handwoven in blues,
lavender, Ming green, Persian
turquoise, peach, sienna, vanilla,

and biscuit
Area rug Repeats colors above, by
Leonard Fisher
Porcelain lamps Jerome Sutter,
Inc.
Lamp stands Jerome Sutter, Inc.
Designed by Kirk White
Director of Design for Sperry and
Hutchinson

Page 146

Ted Ashley, Chairman
Warner Brothers, Inc.
Burbank, California

Entrance Hall
Wall shelf John Mascheroni
Wall fabric Clarence House
Door to Mr. Ashley's office Art
deco

Page 147

Office
Desk Stainless steel top, glass
base; made in Paris by Maria
Peregay
Desk chair Ward Bennett for
Brickel
Pull-up chairs Brno, Knoll
International
Rug Elephant rug; Helene Pollock,
L.A.
Wall light fixtures Art deco, made
in South America; from J. Spector
Imports
Ceiling light fixture Three-tiered
fixtured part of Jack Warner's
original office
Mirror Made from two art deco
headboards; from Newell Galleries,
N.Y.
Swivel lounge chair Ward Bennett
for Brickel
Pull-up armchairs Art deco, from
Newell Galleries, N.Y.; covered in
red mohair from Clarence House
Table between pull-up chairs Four
Seasons, N.Y.
Coffee table Black glass with glass
top; John Mascheroni, N.Y.
Wall covering Gray flannel, from
Vice Versa
Wall cabinet Art deco, brass; from
Newell Galleries (Sony Color TV
installed inside, swivels for viewing
by remote control)
Painting 5 Women, by Norman
Sunshine
Designed by Tom H. John
1355 N. Laurel Avenue
Los Angeles, California 90046
(213) 273-4274
and
68 West 87th Street
New York, New York 10024
(212) 988-4376

Page 150

National Bank of Tulsa
Tulsa, Oklahoma

Elevator Lobby
Floors Unfilled Travertine marble

Walls White sand float plaster
Wall hanging Jack Youngerman
Sculpture James Rosati, Penine 1
(commissioned)
Curtains Blue silk, Scalamandré

Page 151

Corner Dining Room
Lighting Edison Price
Tables Canadian black granite
with stainless steel bases;
Zographos Limited
Chairs Mies van der Rohe, Brno;
special wool fabric by Scalamandré
Carpet Vsoske
Wool casement curtains
Scalamandré
Wall credenza Carpathian elm
burl, designed by Wolf Associates,
executed by Walter P. Sauer and
Sons, Cabinetmakers
Designed by Wolf Associates
Architecture/Interior Design/
Planning
213 Latta Arcade
Charlotte, North Carolina 28202
(704) 374-1833

Page 152

Reception Area
Wender, Murase & White
New York, New York

Furniture and upholstery Knoll
International
Carpet Gullistan Hollyridge
Paneling American elm, designed
by Kliment & Halsband, executed
by B&S Lorch Inc.
Lighting Spun aluminum,
designed by Kliment & Halsband,
and Howard Brandston
Designed by R. M. Kliment &
Frances Halsband, Architects
881 Seventh Avenue
New York, New York 10019
(212) 489-6032

Page 154

Reception Area
The Williams Companies
Tulsa, Oklahoma

Benches Design by Wolf
Associates, in collaboration with
Zographos furniture, Robert John
fabricator. Covered in leather from
American Leather Company
Floor Verde Acceglio marble with
bands of Saint Florient Rose
marble
Wall panels Covered in raw silk by
Far Eastern Fabrics, Inc.
Railing of staircase Brass railing
designed by Wolf Associates,
fabricated by Zephyr Metalcraft.
Structural design by Skilling, Helle,
Christenson and Robertson,
Consulting Engineers
Fountain pool Designed by Wolf
Associates, fabricated by Italmar.
Installed by Oklahoma Tile

Company. Landscape consultant, Arnold Associates. Planting installation by Colmia Nurseries
Designed by Wolf Associates Architecture/Interior Design/ Planning
213 Latta Arcade
Charlotte, North Carolina 28202
(704) 374-1833

Page 156

Ronald Saypol, President
Lionel Corporation
New York, New York

Office
Desk Karl Springer
Desk chair Pace
Rug Patterson, Flynn & Martin, Hi/low Taupe
Fabrics Clarence House
Custom sofa Designed by Robert Metzger, executed by Fine Arts Upholstery
Coffee tables Designed by Robert Metzger, executed by RES Manufacturing Corp.
Tables Designed by Robert Metzger, executed by RES Manufacturing Corp.
Pillow fabric Hand-painted by Peter Fascano

Page 158

Conference Room
Table Karl Springer
Walls Glass block designed by Robert Metzger, executed by Pittsburgh Plate Glass
Chairs Pace Gallery
Rug Patterson, Flynn & Martin
Designed by Robert Metzger Interiors
275 Central Park West
New York, New York
(212) 799-6740

Pages 160–161

Barbini, at Lighting Associates
Hanging lamp
Saline-etched glass with burgundy top and border
Indo #205
H: 11″ D: 22″
Price: Approximately $660

Page 162

Barbini, at Lighting Associates
Spiro table lamp
White hand-blown glass, saline-etched glass column of gray/black
BT #121
H: 20″ D: 15″
Price: Approximately $720

Page 163

Atelier International
Taccia table lamp
Enameled spun aluminum with concave reflector resting on clear

glass bowl. Base housing bulb of aluminum. Finishes: reflector white enamel, black enamel, or sand-blasted natural aluminum Item #F38
H: 21.2″ D: 19.3″
Designed by Castiglioni, 1961
Price: Approximately $700

Page 164

Castelli Furniture
Sintesi Professional lamp
Adjustable and extendable table or wall lamp; diffusor in anodized aluminum with black metal grill
H: 22″
Price: Approximately $95

Page 165

Barbini, at Lighting Associates
BT 103B Aurora
Saline-etched glass
H: 10″ D: 10″
Price: Approximately $460

Accessories

Page 168

Malcolm S. Forbes, President and Editor-in-Chief
Forbes Magazine
New York, New York

Office
Georgian partners' desk Late 18th century, inlaid leather top
Wing chair Chippendale-style, upholstered in red top-grain leather
Pull-up chairs Pair of English 18th century Queen Anne mahogany corner chairs, upholstered in top-grain leather
Card and pencil holders Nephrite; by Fabergé
Crystal-vased flowers Created for Cartier in the 1950s (made of semiprecious stones)
Architect's model of Old Battersea House (adjacent to the wing chair) 17th-century Thames-side mansion restored by Forbes Inc. and now the headquarters of Forbes Europe
Paintings include Bradshaw Krandell's portrait of Forbes founder B. C. Forbes; Sir Joshua Reynolds' very early portrait of Lord Massereene; reduced reproductions of John Koch's two portraits of the Malcolm S. Forbes family (1956 and 1966); Howard Pyle's *On the Beach*; George Bellows' evocative lithograph *Stag at Sharkey's*; James Bama's *Portrait of Dee*; Jean Leon Gérome's *Ils Conspirent*; Jean Renoir's *Baigneuse se Deshabillant*; and Claudio Bravo's *Cabeza de Marro Gui*
Designed by Milholland & Olson, Inc.
8 Stockton Street

Princeton, New Jersey 08540
(609) 924-2175

Page 170

Wine Cellar
Stirrup cups on ceiling beams Tiffany & Co.
Grilled door Spanish monastery from the 16th century
Refectory table Italian, 16th century
Plexiglass chairs Italian, 20th century

Page 171

Dining Room
China 19th-century Bavarian porcelain, hand-painted
Silver-gilt flatware Peter Carl Fabergé, Russian court jeweler
Painting Edward Melcarth, late American realist, unusual presentation of the Last Supper
Porcelains in the vitrine 19th-century copies after Meissen designs
Tables and chairs Knoll International
Designed by Milholland & Olson, Inc
8 Stockton Street
Princeton, New Jersey 08540
(609) 924-2175

Page 172

Halston, President
Halston Enterprises, Inc.
New York, New York

Table and telephone cube Charles Pfister, Knoll International; red lacquer
Chairs Charles Pfister, Knoll International
Carpet Halston, for Karastan
Accessories Elsa Peretti silver objects (pen rest, candlestick, ashtray)
Clock Tiffany & Co.
Orchids Tommy Pashun
Designed by Halston in collaboration with Gruzen & Partners
11 West 42nd Street
New York, New York 10036
(212) 840-3940

Page 176

Conference Room
Bracewell & Patterson,
Attorneys at Law
Houston, Texas

Rug Dhurrie; Stark Carpets, N.Y.
Telescope Philip W. Pfeifer
Designed by Herbert Wells, A.S.I.D
Wells Design Inc.
4314 Westheimer Road
Houston, Texas 77027
(713) 627-0780
Space Planning Caudill Rowlett Scott
1111 West Loop South
Houston, Texas 77027

Linda Pinto, Lead Designer
(713) 621-9600

Page 178

John H. Johnson, President and Publisher
Johnson Publishing Co., Inc.
Chicago, Illinois

Office
Desk Custom-designed walnut burl and bronze lacquer, by Arthur Elrod Associates
Sofa and chair upholstery Maria Kipp, L.A.
Coffee table Arthur Elrod design, walnut and black glass
Walls Behind desk, tortoise-shell lacquer; other walls, suede leather in parquet pattern
Rugs Edward Fields
Window treatment Jack Lenor Larsen

Page 180

Exercise Room
Wall covering Custom-colored red; Connaissance, N.Y.
Carpeting Tretford, N.Y.
Exercise equipment Paramount Health Equipment, L.A.
Basin and plumbing fixtures Sherle Wagner
Barber chair Olson Supply Co., L.A.
Mirrors Parenti & Raffaelli (contractors), Chicago
Upholstery Red vinyl on barber chair and equipment, Pacific Hide & Leather, L.A.
Towels Shaxted, Beverly Hills
Designed by Harold Broderick for Arthur Elrod Associates
850 North Palm Canyon Drive
Palm Springs, California 92262
(714) 325-2593

Page 182

Edward Lee Cave, Senior Vice President
Sotheby Parke Bernet Inc., and Chairman Sotheby's International Realty Corp.
New York, New York

Table Chinese hardwood, c. 1820; frieze carved with strapwork on open fretwork legs
Sideboard George III mahogany, c. 1810
Wing chair George III–style mahogany with scrolled wings, cabriole legs
Chairs Pair of Edwardian mahogany library chairs
Settee George III–style mahogany with camel back, upholstered in wine silk damask
Table Glass and tea paper, entirely covered with glass panels
Screens Pair of six-panel low Japanese screens painted with

trees, waves, and clouds on gold ground
Paintings Chinese reverse painting on glass, lady in ribboned hat, early 19th century; collection of the late Arthur J. Sussel, Philadelphia. *Abandoned Farm, Afternoon, Gordes* and *Country Scene, Provence,* by Van Day Truex, ink and wash, 1963
Carpet Hamadan, in shades of rose, brown, gold and red
Stool Thebes stool, from Liberty of London
Relief Fragmentary Roman marble relief of torso of a reclining male figure
Sheep Stuffed sheep awaiting pick up by forgetful visitor and not a part of Mr. Cave's collection
Walls Red lacquer paint
Sculpture behind desk English 19th-century tobacconist's figure of an Arab

Page 184

Jack Nash, Chairman
Oppenheimer & Co. Inc.
New York, New York

Desk Pilot Woodworking Co., Inc.
Paneling Pilot Woodworking Co., Inc.
Area rug Ernest Treganowan
Floor tile Furstenberg & Co.
Sofas Atelier International, Ltd.
Sofa upholstery leather American Leather Co.
Desk chair Herman Miller Furniture
Recessed lighting Gotham Lighting
Print Robert Rauschenberg
Designed by The Miller Organization Inc., Designers 545 Fifth Avenue
New York, New York 10017
(212) 687-4321

Page 186

Executive Washroom
Murjani International
New York, New York

Drywall and ceiling construction Primo Construction
Ceiling texture and paint Marty Scharfman
Vanity Commercial Cabinet Corp.
Shelves Abacus Plastics
Accessories Signature Settings
Electrical work Nibor Electric, Lightolier
Tile work Ceramica Mia
Plumbing fixtures Kohler, by Stone Supply
Designed by Milo Kleinberg Design Associates, Inc.
633 Third Avenue
New York, New York 10017
(212) 490-2950

Page 188

Arthur Rubloff, Chairman
Rubloff Development Corporation
Chicago, Illinois

Office
Floors Brazilian rosewood parquet
Desk Rosewood and marble
Bronzes Include works by Remington (cast by the Roman Bronze Works): *The Rattlesnake,* 24″ high; *The Cheyenne,* 20″ high; *The Bronco Buster,* 22½″ high. Also bronzes by Dallin, Humphreys and Proctor
Carpet Edward Fields
Oriental rug Tabriz
Coffee table Chinese, over 200 years old
Crystal ball on coffee table Asprey's, London
Glass ashtrays on coffee table Baccarat

Page 190

Dining Room
Linen Handmade by Franklin Bayer, Chicago
China Royal Crown Derby bone china, "Bali" pattern
Crystal Waterford
Flatware Danish stainless steel, Pfeiffer Mangasil
Dining table centerpieces Hen and rooster, Carole Stupell Ltd.
Elephant Bronze, over 150 years old
Paperweight collections Case right houses modern American paperweights; left (not shown in photo), antique French glass paperweights (St. Louis, Clichy, and Baccarat)

Page 192

The Very Reverend James Parks Morton, Dean
Cathedral of St. John the Divine
New York, New York

Rug Semi-antique Heriz
Refectory table Late-16th-century Spanish (gift of Emmy Day)
Framed photographs By Beverly Hall and Ulli Steltzer
Bowls Bernard Leach
Rocks Gathered by Dean Morton in East Hampton and the Sangre de Cristo Mountains in Colorado

Page 194

Alfred Dunhill of London, Inc. Beverly Hills, San Francisco, Chicago, Dallas, Houston, Atlanta, Washington D.C., Bloomingdale's/N.Y.C., Macy's/San Francisco
Slim English attaché
Golden-tan calfskin
Price: Approximately $525

Page 195

Top
Mädler Park Avenue, Inc.
Item #609
17″ x 12½″
Calfskin, suede lined, with combination lock, pocket for paper and pen
Brown, black, burgundy, kast
Price: Approximately $650

Second and third from top
Bottega Veneta
Item #1002
13″ x 17½″
Pressed calf, lined in suede pigskin, with combination lock, pen holder, legal-size file system inside
Tobacco, burgundy, black, green
Price: Under $375
Bottom
Gucci Shops
Teak calf briefcase with front flap closing
Item #015-001-651
Price: Approximately $650

Page 196

Top left
T. Anthony Ltd.
Atlas 7473
Leather inside and out with Irish hand belting, solid brass 24 karat gold plated locks
Dark brown
Price: Under $450

Top right
Lancel
Envelope briefcase
Item #09 30 69
Bordeau
Price: Under $150

Bottom left
Bottega Veneta
Limited Edition Folio
Item #1130
10½″ x 15″
Woven leather folio, opens like a book; leather lined, two pockets
Dark brown
Price: Approximately $550

Bottom right
Bottega Veneta
Item #1111
12″ x 17″
Pressed calf portfolio with contrasting lining, two pockets and a pen holder
Tobacco, burgundy, black, green, dark brown
Price: Approximately $300

Page 197

Top left
Mark Cross, Inc.
Item #94
Brown pigskin, lined in natural

pigskin
Price: Under $600

Top right
Mädler Park Avenue
Item #382
16½″ x 12″
Four compartments and very wide expansion inside zip and outside back pocket
Price: Approximately $650

Bottom left
Mädler Park Avenue
Item #289
16″ x 11½″
Inside zipper compartment and 3-pocket compartment, outside pocket in back
Kast, black, brown, burgundy
Price: Under $350

Bottom right
Hermès, at Bergdorf Goodman
Sac à Dépêches
Black calf
Price: Approximately $2000

Page 198

Top left
Mark Cross
Item #580/16
Memo pad
Russet leather calf
Price: Over $100

Top middle
T. Anthony Ltd.
Manuscript book
Item #6321 Filo
6″ x 9″
Hand-rubbed Venetian calf, burgundy leather bound, blank vellum page
Price: Under $100

Top right
ffolio 72
Address book
7½″ x 9″
Blue cockerill with blue leather trim
Price: Under $35

Middle row, left
ffolio 72
Address book
5½″ x 7″
Gray snake
Price: Approximately $50

Middle row, center
The Economist Newspaper Ltd.
Black wallet diary
Week-at-a-glance type, 2 pockets for money and paper
Price: Approximately $25

Middle row, right
The Economist Newspaper Ltd.
The Economist Diary
10¼″ x 8⅛″ x 1⅜″
120-page section of international

business information
Price: Approximately $45

Bottom left and middle
Bottega Veneta
Agenda, address book, memo pad,
and calculator
8" x 9" x 1½"
In pressed-calf desk or traveling
case, refills available
Item #3143
Price: Under $250
Shown with sterling silver
magnifying glass with ribbed
handle, 2 gold plate bands, for
$155 (Item #6096); sterling silver
felt-tip pen, lizard pattern, with
clip, at $100 (Item #6063); and
sterling silver ballpoint pen, rope
design with gold-plated trim, for
$165 (Item #6067), sold separately

Bottom right
S. T. Dupont
Jotter
China-ink black border
Saks Fifth Avenue, Lord & Taylor,
Bloomingdale's
Item #50011
Price: Approximately $75

Page 199

Top left
Bottega Veneta
Memorandum and address book
Item #3148
6½" x 8¾"
Pressed calf, snap closing, refills
available
Price: Under $100

Top center
T. Anthony Ltd.
Manila-style envelope
Letter size, in burgundy, dark
brown or tan leather
10" x 13"
Price: Approximately $50

Top right
Bulgari
Notepad holder with pen
Item #621044
Sterling silver
Price: Under $500

Middle row, left
Bottega Veneta
Weekly agenda and address book
Item #3100
9" x 11½"
Large size, pressed calf, refills
available
Price: Under $200

Middle row, center
Lancel
Legal-size notepad case
Item #10-30-81
Price: Approximately $80

Middle row, right
Gucci Shops
Phone desk diary

Item #021-116-1330
Combination address book and
appointment calendar; pigskin,
neat metal corners
Price: Approximately $125

Bottom left
Gucci Shops
Executive planner
Item #034-143-58
Address book, diary, and notepad
in pigskin breast-pocket wallet
Price: Under $100

Bottom center
Leathersmith TM of London, Ltd.
Desk organizer and document case
Item #DO1/3H
Envelope style
Price: Approximately $125

Bottom right
ffolio 72
Linen portfolios for desk
Beige with brown, green with green
Price: Approximately $25 each

Page 200

Tiffany & Co.
Alarm clock
Item #4062/54-124
1½" diameter
Gilded brass finish, quartz
movement
Price: Under $200

Page 201

Top left
Concord Watch Corporation
Desk clock
Item #87-533-76
H: 5¼" W: 4⅞" D: 2⅜"
Electric; day date; brushed yellow
brass, polished front plate, silvered
dial
Price: Under $300

Left column, center
Gübelin
Alarm clock
3" x 3"
Jaccard square burgundy lacquer,
8-day movement, gilt and lacquer
finish
Price: Under $150

Bottom left
Tiffany & Co.
Desk clock
Item #9062/53-247
Quartz, gilt finish with brushed
silver dial, alarm
Price: Under $200

Middle column, top
Concord Watch Corporation
Ring clock
Item #82-182-76
2⅜" diameter
Polished yellow brass, 8-day
movement with alarm
Price: Under $250

Middle column, center
Hermès
Infante
Item #1074
3" x 3"
Oval, set in tortoise shell
Price: Approximately $600

Middle column, bottom
Tiffany & Co.
Square alarm clock
Item #9059-1-200
3" x 3"
Gilt with red numbers, 8 day, 15
jewel, alarm
Price: Approximately $150

Top right
Gübelin
Octagonal clock
3" x 3"
Gray lacquer, 8-day movement, gilt
and lacquer finish
Price: Under $150

Right column, center
Van Cleef & Arpels Inc.
Palm Beach, Beverly Hills
Alarm clock
Item #33V171-4
3" diameter
Chrome and gold plated, brushed
silver dial
Price: Approximately $650

Bottom right
Cartier, Inc.
Palm Beach, Houston, Beverly Hills
Square travel clock
Item #57-61232
3" x 3"
Burgundy enamel, brass overlay, 8
day, wind alarm
Price: Approximately $250

Page 202

Right
Tiffany & Co.
Patek Philippe Naviquartz marine
chronometer in case
Item #9063/2-25
5" x 6½"
Mahogany with brass corners and
two incut brass plates
Price: Approximately $3500

Left
Case for clock

Page 203

Left
Tiffany & Co.
Baume & Mercier carriage clock
Item #9069/4-103
3½" x 1½"
Octagonal chronometer in
pearwood case with brass fittings,
octagonal inscription plate inside
top, pigskin carrying case
Price: Approximately $3000

Right
Case for clock

Page 204

Left
Gübelin
Fountain pen
18 karat yellow gold, handmade
bark finish
Price: Under $1500

Top right
A. T. Cross Company
Pen and pencil
Item #8001
Solid 14 karat gold
Price: $1000

Right, second from top
Bulgari
Felt-tip pen
Item #760657/1
18 karat rolled gold on sterling
silver
Price: Approximately $230

Right, third from top
Bulgari
Ruler pen
Item #760702
18 karat gold, extendable to 36
inches, 2 ink colors
Price: Approximately $2000

Bottom right
S. T. Dupont
Fountain pen
18 karat gold nib; black Chinese
lacquer case
Item #46274
Price: Approximately $300

Middle
Mont Blanc Diplomat
In New York available through
Alfred Dunhill of London, Inc.
and Sam Flax
Classic fountain pen; black with 14
karat gold trim and clip, lifetime
guarantee
Price: Approximately $175

Page 205

Top left
Waterman fountain pen
In New York available at Sam Flax
23.3 karat gold electroplate pen, 18
karat gold nib
Price: Over $60

Left, second from top
Aurora Thesi ballpoint
In New York available at Sam Flax
Flat, very thin gold, made in Italy
Price: Gold, under $200; stainless
steel, under $40

Left, third from top
S. T. Dupont
Fountain pen
Tiger eye, 18 karat gold nib
Item #46281
Price: Approximately $320

Bottom left
Flair

Felt-tip pen
Price: Under 80¢

Top right
Cartier, Inc.
The Santos pen
Ballpoint in stainless steel
Price: Approximately $150

Right, second from top
Sheaffer Targa
In New York available at Sam Flax
Fountain pen; geometric pattern,
14 karat gold nib, body 23 karat
gold electroplate
Price: Under $80

Right, third from top
ffolio 72
Bamboo pens
Large and small
Price: $4 and $5

Bottom right
ffolio 72
Pencil, covered with paper
Price: Under $2

Page 206

Sony
BM-12
Portable dictator
15 oz.
Standard pocket size
Price: Under $370

Page 207

Left
Sony BM-12, close-up (see above)

Right
Sony
BM-500
Microcassette, pocket-size
notetaker
9 oz.
Price: Under $300

Page 208

Left
Dictaphone
Micromite
6½" x 3½"
Uses tiny microcassettes, 60
minutes of dictation on each
cassette; "Q-Alert"
Price: Under $300

Right
Norelco
640 Impromptu
6.5 oz.
5⅛" x 2⅛" x ¾"
The world's smallest, lightest
pocket recorder
Price: Approximately $325

Page 209

Top
Norelco
NT-1 UltraSlim Executive Notetaker
8.2 oz.
5¼" x 2 ⁷⁄₁₆" x ¾"
Price: Approximately $275

Bottom
IBM
Executive recorder
Price: Under $200

Page 210

Far left
James II Galleries at James
Robinson, Inc.
Letter opener
Item #M3115
Carved wood boar's head;
Victorian, c. 1870
Price: Under $100

Top left
James Robinson, Inc.
Letter opener
Item #3372C725 L1755
Silver shell skewer, George III,
London, 1775
Price: Under $750

Left column, center
Gübelin
Letter opener
18 karat gold and stainless steel, 8
inches
Price: Approximately $450

Bottom left
James II Galleries at James
Robinson, Inc.
Paper knife
Victorian, Birmingham, 1889;
silver mounted ivory paper knife
Price: Approximately $375

Top right
Buccellati
bottom: magnifying glass,
bookmark and letter opener;
handmade, 7¾" long
Item #2918
top: letter opener; handmade
sterling silver heavily engraved,
sculptured, baroque style
8½" long
Item #2181

Right column, center
Cartier, Inc.
Letter opener
Item #620097
Sterling silver with 18 karat gold
ribbon work
Price: Approximately $300

Bottom right
James II Galleries at James

Robinson, Inc.
Letter opener
Item: #M3144
Victorian, carved and painted
wood, c. 1875
Price: Under $150

Page 211

Top
James II Galleries at James
Robinson, Inc.
Magnifying glass
Item #M3091
Victorian, c. 1890; shagreen and
ivory handle
Price: Approximately $300

Middle
James II Galleries at James
Robinson, Inc.
Magnifying glass
Item #M3048
Victorian, c. 1885; tortoise and
porcelain handle
Price: Approximately $300

Bottom
James II Galleries at James
Robinson, Inc.
Magnifying glass
Item #M3092/6
Victorian, c. 1870; carved wood
handle
Price: Approximately $300

Page 212

Top left
TSAO Designs Inc.
Pencil holder
Item #PH-1
2" diameter x 4" high
Polished chrome
Price: Approximately $35

Bottom left
Mark Cross
Architectural ruler
Sterling silver
Price: Approximately $700

Middle column, top
James II Galleries at James
Robinson, Inc.
Inkwell
Edwardian silver and enamel;
Birmingham, 1907
Price: Over $400

Middle column, second from top
Mark Cross
Bookmark
Item #CP4675
Gold-plated
Price: Under $30

Middle column, third from top
Bulgari
Bowl/ashtray
Item #620053/9

Modern sterling silver
Price: Approximately $150

Middle column, bottom
Tiffany & Co.
Paperweight
Item #2703/25559
2" diameter
Sterling silver sleeping cat
Price: Over $500

Top right
Bulgari
Letter opener
Item #621051/1
Sterling silver and 18 karat gold
inlaid geometric design
Price: Approximately $550

Right column, second from top
Tiffany & Co.
Scotch tape holder
Item #206/552
4" x 5"
Sterling silver
Price: Approximately $650

Right column, third from top
Cartier, Inc.
Letter holder
2½" x 4"
Sterling silver, midnight blue velvet
lining
Price: Under $400

Bottom right
Tiffany & Co.
Openwork gallery tray
Item #534/3422
4" x 5"
Sterling silver
Price: Over $325

Page 213

Top
TSAO Designs Inc.
Ashtray
Item #A-7
7" diameter
Polished greenstone marble,
contemporary square-edge profile
Price: Approximately $50

Middle
TSAO Designs Inc.
Ashtray
Item #CA-91
9" diameter
Mirror-polished chrome finish,
rounded profile
Price: Over $60

Bottom
TSAO Designs Inc.
Ashtray
Item #A-6
6" diameter
Polished black marble, rounded
profile
Price: Under $50

Addresses

Alfred Dunhill of London, Inc.
620 Fifth Ave.
New York, NY 10020
(212) 481-6950

Anthony, T., Ltd.
—See T. Anthony Ltd.

A. T. Cross Company
1 Albion Rd.
Lincoln, RI 02865
(401) 333-1200

Atelier International, Ltd.
595 Madison Ave.
New York, NY 10022
(212) 644-0400

Barbini, at Lighting Associates
—See Lighting Associates

Bernard & S. Dean Levy Inc.
981 Madison Ave.
New York, NY 10021
(212) 628-7088

Bottega Veneta, Inc.
635 Madison Ave.
New York, NY 10021
(212) 371-9218
—Also Beverly Hills

Brickel Associates, Inc.
515 Madison Ave.
New York, NY 10022
(212) 688-2233

Buccellati, Inc.
703 Fifth Ave.
New York, NY 10022
(212) 755-4975

Bulgari
2 E. 61st St.
New York, NY 10021
(212) 486-0086

Cartier, Inc.
653 Fifth Ave.
New York, NY 10022
(212) 753-0111
—Also Houston, Bal Harbour,
Beverly Hills

Castelli Furniture, Inc.
950 Third Ave.
New York, NY 10022
(212) 751-2050

Concord Watch Corporation
—See North American Watch
Corporation

Cross, A. T., Company
—See A. T. Cross Company

Cross, Mark, Inc.
—See Mark Cross, Inc.

Didier Aaron, Inc.
32 E. 67th St.
New York, NY 10021
(212) 988-5248

Dunbar Furniture Corporation
601 South Fulton St.
Berne, IN 46711
(219) 589-2111

Dunhill, Alfred, of London, Inc.
—See Alfred Dunhill of London,
Inc.

Dupont, S. T.
—See S. T. Dupont

The Economist Newspaper Ltd.
75 Rockefeller Plaza
New York, NY 10019
(212) 541-5730

ffolio 72
888 Madison Ave.
New York, NY 10021
(212) 879-0675

Flax, Sam
—See Sam Flax

Florian Papp Inc.
962 Madison Ave.
New York, NY 10021
(212) BU8-6770

Gübelin, Inc.
745 Fifth Ave.
New York, NY 10151
(212) 755-0054

Gucci Shops, Inc.
685 Fifth Ave.
New York, NY 10022
(212) 826-2600
—Also Beverly Hills,
Palm Beach, Bal Harbour,
Chicago
Toll-free line:
(800) 221-2590

Hermès Boutiques
745 Fifth Ave.
New York, NY 10022
(212) 751-3181
—Also Beverly Hills, Chicago,
Palm Beach, Miami

Hyde Park Antiques, Ltd.
818 Broadway
New York, NY 10003
(212) 477-0033

The Incurable Collector, a
subsidiary of Stair & Company
Inc.
42 E. 57th St.
New York, NY. 10022
(212) 755-0140
—See also Stair & Company Inc.

Jack Lenor Larsen, Inc.
232 E. 59th St.
New York, NY 10022
(212) 674-3993

James Robinson, Inc.
15 E. 57th St.
New York, NY 10022
(212) 752-6166

James II Galleries at James
Robinson, Inc.
—See James Robinson, Inc.

Jordan-Volpe Gallery
457 W. Broadway
New York, NY 10012
(212) 533-3900

Kagan, Vladimir, Designs, Inc.
—See Vladimir Kagan Designs, Inc.

Karl Springer Ltd.
306 E. 61st St.
New York, NY 10021
(212) 752-1695

Kittinger Furniture Company
1893 Elmwood Ave.
Buffalo, NY 14207
(716) 876-1000

Knoll International
655 Madison Ave.
New York, NY 10021
(212) 826-2400

Lancel
690 Madison Ave.
New York, NY 10021
(212) 753-6918

Larsen, Jack Lenor
—See Jack Lenor Larsen

Leathersmith of London, Ltd.
3 E. 48th St.
New York, NY 10017
(212) 752-2690

Levy, Bernard & S. Dean, Inc.
—See Bernard & S. Dean Levy Inc.

Lighting Associates, Inc.
305 E. 63rd St.
New York, NY 10021
(212) 751-0575

Mädler Park Avenue
450 Park Ave.
New York, NY 10022
(212) 688-5045

Mark Cross, Inc.
645 Fifth Ave.
New York, NY 10022
(212) 421-3000
—Also Atlanta, Bal Harbour, FL,
Boston, Costa Mesa, CA, Detroit,
Houston, Palm Beach, San
Francisco, Troy, MI.

North American Watch
Corporation
650 Fifth Ave.
New York, NY 10019
(212) 397-7800

Papp, Florian, Inc.
—See Florian Papp Inc.

Robinson, James, Inc.
—See James Robinson, Inc.

Sam Flax and Co.
551 Madison Ave.
New York, NY 10011
(212) 620-3050

Smith & Watson Inc.
305 E. 63rd St.
New York, NY 10021
(212) 355-5615

Springer, Karl
—See Karl Springer

Stair & Company Inc.
59 E. 57th St.
New York, NY 10022
(212) 355-7620

S. T. Dupont
55 Cambridge Parkway
Cambridge, MA 02142
(617) 492-7676

Sunar
18 Marshall St.
Norwalk, CT 06854
(203) 866-3100

T. Anthony Ltd.
480 Park Ave.
New York, NY 10022
(212) 750-9797

Thonet Industries, Inc.
P.O. Box 1587
York, PA 17405
(717) 845-6666

Tiffany & Co.
Fifth Ave. at 57th St.
New York, NY 10022
(212) 755-8000
—Also San Francisco, Beverly Hills,
Houston, Chicago, Atlanta

TSAO Designs Inc.
31 Grove St.
New Canaan, CT 06840
(203) 966-5528

Van Cleef & Arpels Inc.
744 Fifth Ave.
New York, NY 10019
(212) 644-9500

Vladimir Kagan Designs, Inc.
232 E. 59th St.
New York, NY 10022
(212) 371-1512

Ward Bennett Designs for Brickel
Associates Inc.
—See Brickel Associates Inc.

Wood & Hogan, Inc.
305 E. 63rd St.
New York, NY 10021
(212) 355-1335

Zographos Designs Limited
150 E. 58th St.
New York, NY 10022
(212) 421-6650